Unhomed

GLOBAL LIBRARY

Using the image of being "at-home" or "unhomed," Samson Uytanlet traces the narrative of the apostle Paul through Acts, drawing on relevant parts of Paul's letters to highlight this theme. Apart from showing that ultimately Paul is at home in the Lord, this study provokes and challenges Christians today to rethink biblically where we really are at home, challenging us to hospitality, costly discipleship, and living in confident hope. I thoroughly recommend this stimulating book.

Paul Barker, PhD
Visiting Lecturer, Seminari Theoloji Malaysia
Bishop, Anglican Diocese of Melbourne, Australia

One of the most compelling aspects of this book is Samson Uytanlet's exploration of the apostle Paul's life, particularly his experiences of being both unhomed and at-home. Through Paul's own transformation, Uytanlet brings to light the struggles that many of us face today: living in a world where we often feel displaced, yet constantly drawing strength and identity from the secure place we find in Christ. This book beautifully highlights how Paul's encounter with Christ redefined his understanding of power, status, and belonging – principles that resonate powerfully with today's Christians, especially those in ministry.

A central theme in this book is the idea of unhomedness within the early Christian experience. Just as Paul faced rejection and persecution, we too can feel alienated in our walk with Christ. However, it is precisely in this sense of being unhomed that we are drawn closer to Christ, finding our ultimate home in him. Uytanlet's message here is both a source of comfort and challenge for anyone struggling with the tension of belonging in a world that often rejects the message of Christ.

What makes this book so timely and relevant is its practical application to today's Christian life and ministry. Uytanlet's deep theological insights are paired with reflections on how we can live these truths in our daily lives. This is more than an academic work, it is a call for every believer to embrace the journey of being unhomed as a way of experiencing the fullness of God's presence.

Melchor C. Go, DMin
Chancellor,
Asian Theological Seminary, Philippines

This volume is a significant addition to the growing literature on diaspora based on biblical, historical, and autobiographical records. It is not to be kept in dark and dusty bookshelves! Student scholars, local church workers, and mission practitioners need to apply what they learn from the life of Paul during these tumultuous days when millions are uprooted from their homeland and scattered all over the globe. Consequently, they are looking for a new home. Samson Uytanlet's work deserves serious study!

Sadiri Joy Tira, DMiss, DMin
Diaspora Missiology Specialist,
Jaffray Centre for Global Initiatives,
Ambrose University, Canada

The Christian life is one of having to come home to God through Christ and becoming a pilgrim. It is being found by God and being on the road of witness and service. It is living faith's security and faith's challenges in being salt, light, and leaven in the world. This double movement of the Christian life has been grounded by Samson Uytanlet in Luke's Acts narrative of the life and mission of Paul. With both disciplined and creative exegetical skill, Paul's life of service in and for Christ has been sculpted by the metaphors of being at home and being unhomed. Expressing the whole gamut of Paul's missional experience of new life in Christ and that of welcome and community, as well as that of conflict and rejection, these metaphors are as helpful as ever in living the faith in the twenty-first century. As such, this understanding of the Christian life forms a sharp contrast to all forms of easy believe-ism, a prosperity gospel, and a faith without conflict and resistance. This book is an important challenge to the contemporary church.

Charles Ringma, PhD
Emeritus Professor, Regent College, Canada
Research Professor, Asian Theological Seminary, Philippines

Unhomed

Paul's Journey In Between Hostility and Hospitality

Samson L. Uytanlet

© 2025 Samson L. Uytanlet

Published 2025 by Langham Global Library
An imprint of Langham Publishing
www.langhampublishing.org

Langham Publishing and its imprints are a ministry of Langham Partnership

Langham Partnership
PO Box 296, Carlisle, Cumbria, CA3 9WZ, UK
www.langham.org

ISBNs:
978-1-78641-230-0 Print
978-1-78641-250-8 ePub
978-1-78641-251-5 PDF

Samson L. Uytanlet has asserted his right under the Copyright, Designs and Patents Act, 1988 to be identified as the Author of this work.

All rights reserved. No part of this publication may be reproduced, stored in a retrieval system or transmitted, in any form or by any means, electronic, mechanical, photocopying, recording or otherwise, without the prior written permission of the publisher or the Copyright Licensing Agency.

Requests to reuse content from Langham Publishing are processed through PLSclear. Please visit www.plsclear.com to complete your request.

All Scripture quotations, unless otherwise indicated, are taken from The Holy Bible, English Standard Version® (ESV®), copyright © 2001 by Crossway, a publishing ministry of Good News Publishers. Used by permission. All rights reserved.

Scripture quotations marked (NASB) are taken from the New American Standard Bible®, Copyright © 1960, 1962, 1963,1968, 1971, 1972, 1973, 1975, 1977, 1995, 2020 by The Lockman Foundation. Used by permission.

British Library Cataloguing-in-Publication Data
A catalogue record for this book is available from the British Library

ISBN: 978-1-78641-230-0

Cover & Book Design: projectluz.com

Langham Partnership actively supports theological dialogue and an author's right to publish but does not necessarily endorse the views and opinions set forth here or in works referenced within this publication, nor can we guarantee technical and grammatical correctness. Langham Partnership does not accept any responsibility or liability to persons or property as a consequence of the reading, use or interpretation of its published content.

In memory of my mother-in-law,
Lily Soo
(1945–2025)

Contents

	Foreword	xi
	Preface	xiii
1	Ambivalently Unhomed	1
2	A Jew At-Home in the Diaspora	7
3	Unhomed Follower of the Way	23
4	Unhomed Missionary to Galatia	37
5	Unhomed Missionary to Greece and Asia Minor	57
6	Housed in a Prison, Imprisoned in a House, Still Unhomed	85
7	Unhomed with Human Power, At-Home with Divine Presence	107
	Bibliography	113
	Subject Index	119
	Author Index	123
	Scripture Index	125

Foreword

The cry of the human heart is to feel at home with one's self, one's community, and most of all, with God. It is rooted in human identity as the beloved. We want to belong and be ourselves in the truth of who we are. Others want to fix us in their own ways instead of allowing us freedom. Instead of respecting others' perspectives and practices of living and serving God, they lord it over us and others. Instead of inclusion, the culture of exclusion makes many people "unhomed" in their families and friends, churches, and communities.

One of the most painful experiences in being unhomed is rejection. We can understand the secular culture, which thrives in competition and comparison, leading to the experience of being unhomed in human society but, sadly, rejection is also alive in Christian communities that set aside respect and reception. Christ has abolished "the dividing wall of hostility." He has created a new humanity where religion and race, sexuality and status, color and class are redeemed in Christ (Eph 2:14–18; Gal 3:26–28; Col 3:11). Yet what Jesus took to the cross is celebrated in many churches today. Many women leaders are unhomed in their denominations. Colored people are discriminated as second class humans. Those who struggle in their sexuality are condemned rather than given a space of compassion. Many young people are unhomed in churches that do not understand their generation.

Many pastors I mentor and minister feel unhomed. They are forced to project an image of acceptance even if their worlds are falling apart. They have no real friends for them to share their inner struggle. They do not feel safe and secure to be at home with what they are going through for fear of being misunderstood and marginalized. Many pastors consider their own local churches and denominations the most unsafe places for them to be who they really are. Consequently, they are unhomed as they project an impressive appearance of pleasing people in exchange for their praises.

Mentoring is offering a safe place with secure people to feel at home. Mentors offer a hospitality of grace so mentees feel welcomed. We give mentees hearing space to share their secret struggle(s) without the fear of rejection. The homey place creates an environment for pastors to be the beloved and to claim their true identity in Christ.

In a success-driven ministry, many pastors feel unhomed, especially those serving in small churches. Paul confronted this head on in Philippians 3:1–11.

When we've worked to build great things, these works are mere garbage – in fact, they are "dog dung" (*The Message* version). Mentoring helps pastors move from feeling unhomed to feeling at home. It is a process of shifting to leadership where character matters more than credentials, credibility more than charisma, and fellowshipping with the crucified is more prized than the fan club of celebrity. This calls for dying to the false self and rising with the new self in Christ. It happens in the climate of grace to live in the home of love.

The theme of unhomed from Paul's missionary work and experience as a Christian evangelist is critical for our continuing reflection, not just in ministry but more so in spirituality. Paul preached and practised the gospel of grace; that by grace we can be at home with our weaknesses and wounds as we simultaneously experience God's healing and help (2 Cor 12:7–10). The unhomed can be at home in the church of broken people being formed in the beauty of Christ (2 Cor 4:7–12). It is when pastors and church leaders learn to accept their human failure and frailty that they can minister to the unhomed.

Deep in the human soul is the longing for home. In this life, we will remain unhomed for this is not our true home. Like Abraham, we look and long for a true home whose maker and builder is God (Heb 11:10). Meanwhile we live as unhomed, "strangers in a foreign country" (v. 9) until we enter the eternal home where God dwells (Heb 13:14–15). Our true home is hidden in Christ (Col 3:3) in our hearts which have become the home of the Triune God. We need to cultivate the feeling of being unhomed in this world to keep seeking our true home in the kingdom of God. We can only look and long for our true spiritual home and to rest in God's love after we have seriously embraced our being unhomed in this world.

Samson Uytanlet has given us a scholarly excursion to wrestle with Paul's experience of being unhomed and at home in the presence of God and with a few people who became Paul's faithful friends in life and ministry. It is not a simple book to read; it is a very substantial and significant aid for developing a ministry rooted in grace that offers a place like home, where believers are safe and secure to be authentic people growing in the image of Christ. This book is not just for scholars but for every servant leader who thinks biblically and reflects theologically on the process of developing a community of love where unhomed people become at home. Those who read and reflect on this book can relate to its message and see its relevance to serve the many unhomed in their communities. The gospel is a way to come home to God in Jesus Christ.

Herman Moldez, Senior Pastor
Faith Baptist Church, Quezon City, Philippines

Preface

After publishing our first book together, the *Manual for Sojourners* (henceforth *Manual*),[1] my wife, Juliet, and I thought that it would be good to follow it up with another volume on a similar theme. Originally, the *Manual* was the thesis I submitted to complete my Master of Theology. The year that I graduated was the same year we married – not knowing that years later she would be involved with the Global Diaspora Network (GDN) of the Lausanne Movement. Within the two years that she served as a catalyst for the GDN, we thought it would be an appropriate time to produce something related to the issue of diaspora. To complete that work, I revised and updated the aforementioned thesis, which focuses primarily on the text of 1 Peter, and Juliet provided suitable materials related to contemporary diaspora and to the issues addressed by Peter. The *Manual* took us several years to complete, despite its brevity. The idea began in 2016 and was finally published 2023 (the period would be longer if we count the years between the year of my thesis defense in 2002 and the publication of its revised and updated version).

In the course of our discussions as we produced the *Manual*, she introduced me to the works of Homi K. Bhabha and his idea of the "unhomely." These created interest in producing another work after the *Manual*, but instead of focusing on the experiences of diasporan believers in general, the focus would be on the experiences of Christian ministers who are constantly on the move, like journeyman athletes, who go through the experience of ambivalence, of belonging and not belonging, of experiencing hospitality and hostility within the same group of people, of being honored and disgraced for their work, and of being at home and unhomed in their places of ministry all at the same time. With this in mind, it seemed that a biographical study of Paul was a good place to start this topic.[2]

In 2023, having received a post-doctoral research grant from Langham Partnership to work on this project, the production of this current work ensued. It is my hope that as we read through the experiences of Paul being at-home and unhomed in the places of his ministry, it will bring encourage-

---

1. Samson Liao Uytanlet and Juliet Lee Uytanlet, *Manual for Sojourners: A Study on Peter's Use of Scripture and Its Relevance Today* (Eugene: Wipf and Stock, 2023).

2. Unless otherwise specified, the English Standard Version is used for this volume.

ment and solace, especially to Christian ministers as they continue doing the work of the Lord.

1

Ambivalently Unhomed

The ancient Greek expression *aoikētos* refers to a place that is uninhabitable.[1] One might expect that the related expression *aoikos* would refer to a *homeless person*, one "without a house," rather than a *"houseless" place* in which no person dwells. However, the expression *aoikos* (literally, "without a house") is also used similarly, referring to a place that is "deserted."[2] These two expressions were also used more broadly in classical Greek writings. The expression *aoikētos* can refer to an uninhabited *place* like the desert or a *person* banished from home and therefore made "homeless"; metaphorically, it alludes to one who is miserable. *Aoikos* also refers to a person, like a foreigner in a village, who is houseless or homeless.[3] A place can be without a person dwelling in it, making it deserted whether it is merely uninhabited or completely uninhabitable; and a person can be without a place in which to dwell, making them houseless or homeless. Metaphorically, a person can also be rejected, exiled, driven away from their home, and unwelcomed, making them "unhomed." These expressions show that in ancient Greek thought the concept of being physically present or residing in a place was inevitably tied to the idea of belonging to a community wherein one is welcomed and can give or receive hospitality in its various expressions, and that misery could come as a result of being made homeless or unhomed.

---

1. BDAG, s.v. *aoikētos*. In the version of the story of the Watchers in the Testament of Naphtali 3:5, as a consequence of their sins, God pronounced a curse on the land so that no one would be able to dwell in it. The same expression is also used in the Greek Old Testament (e.g. Deut 13:17; Josh 8:28; 13:3; Hos 13:5; Job 8:14). See James H. Charlesworth, ed., *The Old Testament Pseudepigrapha*, 2 vols. (Garden City: Doubleday, 1983–1985).

2. BDAG, s.v. *aoikos*. The lexical entries for any lexicon are based on its use within a body of available materials for which the lexicon was designed, so in many instances the full range of possible nuances of a word cannot be reflected in the entries.

3. LSJ, s.v. *aoikētos*.

Fast forward to the twentieth century in which synonymous expressions were used in various disciplines to describe this human experience. Within the first quarter of that century, Sigmund Freud published several works on psychoanalysis, one of which was *Das Unheimliche* (literally, "The Unhomely"). This work was later translated to English and was entitled *The Uncanny* by Alix Strachey.[4] Writing from a psychoanalytic perspective, Freud defines the "uncanny" or "unhomely" as "something which is secretly familiar . . . which has undergone repression and then returned from it."[5] The translator of Freud underscores the fact that the common English use of the term "unhomely" is not similar to the neurologist's use of the German word *unheimlich*.[6] Hence, Strachey chose the word "uncanny" to express that in-between state of knowing and not knowing that produces fright.[7] More pertinent to our discussion is Freud's attempt at a definition of the "unhomely" by considering the various nuances of the expression *unheimlich* ("unhomely") and *heimlich* ("homely"). The "unhomely," being the opposite of the "homely" or "familiar," is frightening. The "homely" is more than just a reference to that which belongs to the family. In referring to animals, the adjective describes those that are "tame," an expression used of those that were domesticated, companionable, and often considered part of the human family. The expression *heimlich* or "homely" also carries the idea of being intimate, friendly, comfortable, quiet contentment, agreeable, restful, and secure.[8]

Toward the end of the same century, another work was produced discussing the human state of being "unhomely," but this time from the perspective of postcolonial study of culture. Homi K. Bhabha remarks about the "in-between spaces" wherein one (the colonized) realizes the presence of cultural differences between themselves and the other (the colonizer). He continues, "These 'in-between' spaces provide the terrain for elaborating strategies of selfhood – singular or communal – that initiate new signs of identity."[9] He uses the expres-

---

4. Sigmund Freud, "The Uncanny," in *The Standard Edition of the Complete Psychological Works of Sigmund Freud*, vol. 17, trans. Alix Strachey, ed. James Strachey (London: Hogwarth Press, 1925), 218–53. The original German work was produced in 1919.

5. Freud, "The 'Uncanny,'" 245.

6. Freud, "The 'Uncanny,'" 219, n. 1.

7. Ferial J. Ghazoul explains this ambivalence is experienced when the repressed begin to be recognized, and because it has not been on the surface, it creates a feeling of being both "homely" and "unhomely," of being at home and at the same time not at home. See Ghazoul's "The Unhomely At Home and Abroad," *Journal of Arabic Literature* 35, no. 1 (2004): 2.

8. Freud, "The 'Uncanny,'" 221–22.

9. Homi K. Bhabha, *The Location of Culture* (London: Routledge Classics, 1994), 2.

sion "unhomely" to describe the condition of one who is transitioning from one culture to another, perhaps by imitation, often by the colonized mimicking the colonizer. This cultural relocation is the process of being unhomed. He further explains

> The negating activity is, indeed, the intervention of the "beyond" that establishes a boundary: a bridge, where "presencing" begins because it captures something of the estranging sense of relocation of the home and the world – the unhomeliness – that is the condition of extra-territorial and cross-cultural initiations. To be unhomed is not to be homeless, nor can the "unhomely" be easily accommodated in that familiar division of social life into private and public spheres.[10]

While Freud and Bhabha use the term "unhomely" to convey dissimilar ideas from different vantage points, they see the state of being unhomely as having a characteristic of ambivalence, such as estrangement in engagement, or unfamiliarity even in a state of awareness. In English parlance, to be "at home" means to experience freedom to express oneself, to enjoy hospitality and positive reception, and to feel some familiarity and connection within a group of people. The opposite of this is to be unhomed: instead of experiencing freedom to express, one is suppressed and silenced; instead of enjoying hospitality, one is met with hostility; instead of connection, there is alienation. This is how the expressions "at-home" and "unhomed" will be used as contrasts throughout the chapters.[11]

At-Home with Power, Unhomed for Weaknesses

The experience of being unhomed is common to humans. There is a natural longing among diasporan communities of finding a place to be "at home." This is true for diasporan communities today,[12] but we can assume that ancients

---

10. Bhabha, *The Location of Culture*, 13.

11. Hospitality, as Andrew Spurgeon defines it, "is offering a safe space for the needy (including a stranger, homeless, and refugees), accepting them for who they are, and extending God's provisions and protections to them." See Andrew B. Spurgeon, "Practicing Hospitality: Ancient Cultural Values and the Contemporary Asian Christians," in *Exploring the New Testament in Asia: An Evangelical Perspective*, Foundations in Asian Christian Thought, ed. Samson L. Uytanlet and Bennet Lawrence (Carlisle: Langham Global Library, 2024), 278.

12. Juliet Lee Uytanlet, "Finding Home for the Unhomed: Helping Diaspora Community Discover Identity and Belonging," in *Asian Christian Theology: Evangelical Perspectives*, ed. Timoteo D. Gener and Stephen T. Pardue (Carlisle: Langham Global Library, 2019), 273.

also experienced the same. Even the heroes of the Christian faith, like the apostle Paul, were not exempt from this. His biographical sections in the New Testament show the ways he experienced being at-home and unhomed as a diasporan Jewish missionary who ministered among the Jews in their homeland, the diasporan Jews scattered around the Mediterranean, and the Gentile natives among these host countries.

In Paul's case, the state of ambivalence that we find in these records was not about his repressed thoughts for there is no way we can access them. There might have been cultural exchanges at some points between Paul and the people with whom he was interacting but, for this present work, the focus will be on his experience of being at-home and unhomed by certain groups of people, on being welcomed and rejected as a missionary, and how the latter led to persecution in the form of violence, death threats, attempted murder, and imprisonment.

Luke presented several factors that generated hostile responses to Paul's mission. The first factor originated in differences in theological or doctrinal stances on certain issues. The belief in the resurrection, for instance, was one issue that separated even the two major Jewish religious groups during the first century, namely, the Pharisees and the Sadducees. Like the Pharisees, the early Christians also believed in the resurrection. The Sadducees did not hold to the same view, which explains the tension within the Sanhedrin between the Sadducees and the Pharisees during Paul's trials (Acts 23:6–8) and, in part, the attempt of the priestly elites to silence Peter and John as they preached about the resurrection of Jesus (4:10). The believing Pharisees might have agreed with the followers of Jesus on the resurrection, but they disagreed on the issue of circumcising Gentiles. Disputes regarding theological differences or (to use Christian jargon) "contending for the faith" or "defending the truth," can sometimes be used as a pretext for a claim to power.[13] Losing influence over others can be a strong motivation to ostracize, malign, and silence those who theologically disagree with one, and often even on trivial issues.

Loss of influence and power was one factor, economic and financial losses were others. The new-found faith of the Ephesians caused severe loss to the businesses of the idol craftsmen (19:25–27), leading the members of the guild into a unified effort to attack Paul. Cloaked with a devotion to protect the honor

---

13. Heinrich Schäfer laments that in the modern era, absolutizing one's theological view (even the less essential doctrines or those that are unclear in Scripture), legitimizing it as the only valid one, and stigmatizing changes in *status quo* are ways to claim power and status. See "Fundamentalism: Power and the Absolute," *Exchange* 23, no. 1 (1994): 12. See also Martyn Percy, "Power and Fundamentalism," *Journal of Contemporary Religion* 10, no. 3 (1995): 273–82.

of their goddess, Artemis, the craftsmen found a reason to hide their rage toward Paul for ruining their idol-producing business. The same motivations led the owners of the clairvoyant slave girl into instigating an attack against Paul, resulting in his first recorded imprisonment as a missionary (16:19–24).

Another factor that generated hostility to Paul related to ethnicity. Ethnic tensions were a reality that people in the New Testament (NT) had to face, as observed in the story of the encounter of Jesus with the Samaritan woman (John 4). In Acts, however, belongingness was not so much determined by one's race, but one's spoken language and one's willingness to adhere to external signs of Jewish ethnic identity – both played a role in one's acceptance into and rejection by a group. The Hellenistic Jewish widows were less prioritized in food distribution, not because of their ethnicity or extent of need, but because of the language they spoke (Acts 6:1). The contrast between the "Hellenist widows" and "Hebraists widows" in Acts 6 suggests that the primary reason for prioritizing one group was their language. This tendency is currently seen among other people groups, for example, diasporan Chinese communities, wherein Mandarin speakers are sometimes treated better than those who are unable to speak fluent Mandarin. In some cases, it is the other way around.[14] Among the diasporan Chinese in the United States, English proficiency has also become a marker of social status.[15] The fact that Paul was bilingual gave him an edge among the Jews in their homeland and in the diaspora, but his unwillingness to require Gentiles to bear the physical mark of circumcision and be identified as a "Jew" was unacceptable to some Jews.

Self-preservation and political standing motivated some groups to persecute Paul. We see this in the events in Thessalonica when some Jews believed that Paul's message jeopardized their standing before those who held political power. They interpreted Paul's message as an affront to the Roman emperor's authority because he proclaimed "another king, Jesus" (1 Thess 17:7). This would not have been a problem if the Romans clearly distinguished between Jewish Christians and non-Christians within the same diasporan community and within the same synagogue.

Social status is another factor that can determine whether a person will be welcomed by a group. Wealth is one of the determining factors of social

---

14. Juliet L. Uytanlet, *The Hybrid Tsinoys: The Challenges of Hybridity and Homogeneity as Sociocultural Constructs Among the Chinese in the Philippines*, American Society of Missiology Monograph Series 28 (Eugene: Pickwick, 2016), 97–98.

15. Stephen H. Chen, Emily Zhang, Cindy H. Liu, and Leslie K. Wang, "Depressive Symptoms in Chinese Immigrant Mothers: Relations with Perceptions of Social Status and Interpersonal Support," *Cultural Diversity & Ethnic Minority Psychology* 27, no.1 (2021): 72–81.

status, but it is not the only one. One's education, the people with whom one associates, one's public persona, accomplishments, and eloquence can each raise or diminish one's status. In Paul's case, as he ministered at Corinth he went through a period when his authority as an apostle was challenged, his public demeanor was frowned upon, his abilities were questioned, and as a result, he was abhorred by some who considered themselves high and mighty. This resulted in Paul's rejection by some members of this "elite" community.

Whether we look into doctrinal/theological differences, economic/financial elements, questions on race/ethnicity and language, political standing, or social status, the bottom line of all these factors is power – power that can potentially be gained, power threatened to be lost, and power to be maintained. No wonder Paul operated with one important principle in his ministry, "For the sake of Christ, then, I am content with weaknesses, insults, hardships, persecutions, and calamities. For when I am weak, then I am strong" (2 Cor 12:10).

In this present work, I will examine the life of Paul as narrated by Luke in his sequel to his Gospel, the book of Acts. Information from Acts will be supplemented by data from the autobiographical portions of Paul's letters. After a brief discussion on Paul's ethnic, religious, and educational background in the first chapter, the outline and discussions in the succeeding chapters will follow the order in which Luke recounts the events in the life of Paul, with occasional digressions to Paul's letters to supplement the information presented in Acts.

2

A Jew At-Home in the Diaspora

The exile of the Jews to Babylon is a good starting point for telling Paul's story as one among the hundreds of thousands of Jews in the diaspora. The historian who wrote 1–2 Kings summarized the aftermath of Nebuchadnezzar's siege of Jerusalem and Jehoiachin's surrender to the Babylonians

> He carried away all Jerusalem and all the officials and all the mighty men of valor, 10,000 captives, and all the craftsmen and the smiths. None remained, except the poorest people of the land. And he carried away Jehoiachin to Babylon. The king's mother, the king's wives, his officials, and the chief men of the land he took into captivity from Jerusalem to Babylon. And the king of Babylon brought captive to Babylon all the men of valor, 7,000, and the craftsmen and the metal workers, 1,000, all of them strong and fit for war. (2 Kgs 24:14–16)

According to the Chronicler, this was a fulfillment of Jeremiah's prophecy (2 Chr 36:20–21). Their story did not end in exile, however. God also promised Jeremiah that the exiles would return after seventy years (Jer 25:11–12; 29:10), and later prophets like Daniel saw this fulfilled (Dan 9:2). The descendants of the Jews exiled to Babylon had multiple opportunities to return to Jerusalem, but external records suggest that many of them chose to stay in Mesopotamia and live among the Babylonians. One such record is the letter of Antiochus IV to Zeuxis, wherein the king instructed that two thousand Jewish families be moved from Mesopotamia to Lydia and Phrygia. This decision was made after a sedition took place in these two regions. In the same letter, Antiochus expressed confidence that the Jews, because of their religious piety, would be "guardians" of the possessions of the Greeks. In return, the king promised the Jews freedom to practice their religion, lands to cultivate and raise animals, materials to build their houses, and tax exemption (Josephus, *Jewish Antiquities*

12.3.4 §§148–53). Prior to this event, as Josephus recorded, Seleucus Nicator granted citizenship to the Jews in Asia, Lower Syria, and Antioch, allowing them to be members of the king's auxiliaries (*Jewish Antiquities* 12.3.1 §119).

Migration and relocation continued even after the Persians repopulated the Mediterranean regions with people from other locales. Josephus cited Strabo who observed how the Jews relocated into various cities and made their presence felt (*Jewish Antiquities* 14.7.1 §§114–15).[1] The presence of Jews in various regions north of the Mediterranean is well attested. Not much was said about the Jews in Tarsus, but there is information about Jews from Jerusalem in Iasos who once contributed financially for the festival of Dionysius in Tarsus.[2] Whether this contribution was a sign of devotion to the deity is unclear, but it definitely shows some kind of friendship between the Jews and the Tarsians. This happened in the city where the apostle Paul was born and spent a significant amount of his time as an adult.

Paul of Tarsus

Luke mentions the origin of Paul a few times in his narrative. He was known as Saul when he first appeared in Acts (7:58–8:3; 9:1–31; 11:25–30; 13:1–9) until his encounter with Elymas the magician when Luke began to refer to him as Paul (13:9).[3] In the case of the new African immigrants to the United States, Hewan Girma suggests that personal names can be used to "signify ethnic or religious identity, are useful sociocultural indicators which can encapsulate historical and social processes."[4] While the said study focused on the new African immigrants (particularly Ethiopian-Americans) in contradistinction with the African-Americans (those who were in the country for generations), the reality that names carry ethnic and cultural markers applies to people in any diasporan community. In the episode of Paul's appearance before the Roman tribunal, he claimed to be an ethnic Jew born in Tarsus of Cilicia (22:3). Paul

---

1. Erich S. Gruen, *Diaspora: Jews Amidst Greeks and Romans* (Cambridge: Harvard University Press, 2002), 2.

2. Gruen, *Diaspora*, 130. See also the *Corpus Inscriptionum Judaicarum*, vol. 1, no. 749.

3. For our purposes, unless it is necessary to call him by his original name, Saul, we will mostly refer to him as Paul since this is the name he is usually referred to in writings about him.

4. Hewan Girma, "Black Names, Immigrant Names: Navigating Race and Ethnicity Through Personal Names," *Journal of Black Studies* 51, no. 1 (2020): 16. A similar observation can be made based on the information from the German Socio-Economic Panel regarding Turkish, Southwest European, and former Yugoslav immigrants. See Jürgens Gerhards and Silke Hans, "From Hasan to Herbert: Name-Giving Patterns of Immigrant Parents between Acculturation and Ethnic Maintenance," *American Journal of Sociology* 114, no. 4 (2009): 1102–28.

also mentioned that he studied under Gamaliel, which means that he must have lived in Jerusalem for a significant period of time.[5] There is no record from the ancient rabbis that is equivalent to modern educational curricula: this makes it difficult to determine the age at which Paul went to Jerusalem for his training to become a Pharisee and how much time he spent there before going back to Tarsus. The information in Scripture about Paul's origin and upbringing is meager. Filling the information gaps is a great challenge but it can be inferred from Luke's record that before Paul became a follower of Jesus he was living in Tarsus. Thus, when Ananias received the divine message to pray for Paul's recovery of his sight, he was referred to as "a man of Tarsus named Saul" (9:11). Paul was in Jerusalem at that early stage when the Jerusalem church was becoming multi-ethnic and bilingual (see Acts 6–7) and was present when one of its leaders, Stephen, was executed for proclaiming Christ (7:58–8:1). Paul, who was then Saul, actively persecuted the believers in Jerusalem (8:3) – he even went to the high priest to ask for a letter so he could make the persecution official (9:1–2). After his experience on the road to Damascus, Paul went back to Tarsus (9:26–30) before eventually joining Barnabas in Antioch of Syria, where they were both commissioned as missionaries (13:1–3).

There is no way to ascertain how much time Paul spent in his host city of Tarsus as he was growing up, but it is clear that Paul was a diasporan Jew based on the fact that he spent the last thirty years of his life in the diaspora. As John M. G. Barclay underscores, it was "in this geographical and social context that [Paul's] mission and his new theological reflection took place."[6]

As a Jew who was born in a foreign country, brought up in a traditional Jewish household, exposed to a Greek form of education, studied under a strict Jewish form of training, frequented his homeland, and travelled to and stayed in many Greek cities as a professional tentmaker and vocational preacher of the gospel, there is something about Paul that is "very Greek" and something that is "very Jewish." Hybridity has its advantages. It enabled the apostle to *naturally* be a Jew among Jews and still be one among those "outside the law" (1 Cor 9:21). The extent to which Paul maintained his Jewishness in a foreign land and the extent to which he assimilated, acculturated, and accommodated

---

5. Hence, there was a discussion as to where Paul spent much of his growing years, whether in Tarsus or in Jerusalem as a Pharisee-in-training. See Wilhelm C. van Unnik, *Tarsus or Jerusalem: The City of Paul's Youth* (London: Epworth Press, 1962); Martin Hengel, *The Pre-Christian Paul* (London: SCM Press, 1991).

6. John M. G. Barclay, "Paul Among Diaspora Jews: Anomaly or Apostate?," *Journal for the Study of the New Testament* 18, no. 60 (1996): 90.

the Hellenistic culture and values might have varied depending on the stages and foci of his life.

Barclay explains that, wherever Paul went, he *assimilated* pretty well to the Hellenistic host country except for the practice of idolatry. Assimilation, by definition, is social integration and becoming similar to one's neighbor. The degree to which a Jew assimilated in their Hellenistic host country on Barclay's scale of assimilation ranged from no assimilation (their social life still confined within the Jewish community), to a more moderate form of assimilation (commerce and employment with non-Jews, attendance at Greek athletics or theaters, gymnasium education), to total assimilation (abandonment of key social distinctives).[7] In Paul's case, he (1) defended the propriety of eating with Gentiles against non-Christian Jews (Gal 2:12), (2) promoted liberty on the issue of food consistent with Jesus's stance on the issue (1 Cor 8–10; cf. Mark 7:18–19), (3) redefined intermarriage by accepting inter-ethnic marriages but setting a boundary that marriages must be "in the Lord" (1 Cor 7:39), and (4) acknowledged the cultural value of the "holy kiss" that defies ethnic boundaries (1 Cor 16:20; Rom 16:16). The one thing that kept Paul from fully assimilating was his stance on idolatry.[8]

There are different opinions as to how well Paul *acculturated*. Acculturation refers to the educational aspects of cultural exposure which may range from little to no facility in Greek, to acquaintance with the common moral values, to familiarity with the standard Greek education (including literature, rhetoric, philosophy, and theology), and to scholarly expertise.[9] While Paul admitted to being ineloquent (2 Cor 11:6; cf. 1 Cor 1–4), he could and did use common Hellenistic assessments of the human condition (Rom 7) and Stoic-sounding terms (1 Cor 7:29–31; Phil 4:11).[10] (His education will be discussed in more detail later.)

Paul had assimilated and acculturated well to the Hellenistic environment, but he did not *accommodate* the Greek ideals, refusing to allow them to shape his understanding of his Jewish heritage. For the diasporan Jews, accommodation ranged from antagonism toward the Greco-Roman culture to reinterpretation of Judaism while preserving some uniqueness to total submersion of the Jewish cultural uniqueness.[11] Barclay summarizes,

---

7. Barclay, "Paul Among Diaspora Jews," 93–95.
8. Barclay, "Paul Among Diaspora Jews," 103–4.
9. Barclay, "Paul Among Diaspora Jews," 95–96.
10. Barclay, "Paul Among Diaspora Jews," 104–7.
11. Barclay, "Paul Among Diaspora Jews," 97–98.

An interesting and anomalous phenomenon emerges here, for despite the fact of his relatively high assimilation with Gentiles, Paul's perspective on the world still operates in line with the traditional Scriptural excoriation of Gentiles, only sharpened by his apocalyptic dualism. Paul's most common construction of his world is in terms of the simple biblical division between Jews and "the nations" (τὰ ἔθνη, Gal. 2.8–9 etc.), and if he glosses this occasionally as a contrast between "Jews" and "Greeks," it is as if no Jews could also consider themselves (in cultural terms) "Greek."[12]

Paul: A Jew in the Ancient Roman Society

There is neither a portrait nor a description of Paul's physical appearance from his contemporaries. As Adolf Deissmann observes, "who in that day would have thought of recording his face for the future, when the countenance of the Master Himself even had not been immortalized?"[13] Not much was said about Paul's physical appearance in later writings. One of the few examples is this short excerpt from an apocryphal writing known as the Acts of Paul and Thecla.

> And he went along the road to Lystra and kept looking at the passers-by according to the description of Titus. And he saw Paul coming, a man small in size, bald-headed, bandy-legged, of noble mien, with eyebrows meeting, rather hook-nosed, full of grace. Sometimes he seemed like a man, and sometimes he had the face of an angel. (Acts of Paul and Thecla 3)[14]

This physical description was not flattering at all,[15] but the author of this apocryphal Acts compensated for the disparaging comment by comparing the apostle to an angel. A similar uncomplimentary description was made about Jesus, the servant about whom Isaiah prophesied (Isa 53:2). In the Scripture, much less is mentioned about Paul's physical description. Paul hinted about

---

12. Barclay, "Paul Among Diaspora Jews," 107.
13. Adolf Deissmann, *Paul: A Study in Social and Religious History*, trans. William E. Wilson (New York: Harper & Row, 1957), 55–56.
14. Based on J. K. Elliott, *The Apocryphal New Testament: A Collection of Apocryphal Christian Literature in an English Translation Based on M. R. James*. New York: Oxford University Press, 1993.
15. The description about Paul's nose is the kind of racially prejudiced stereotypes about the Jews prevalent in early modern art and music, as Dan Harrán shows ("The Jewish Nose in Early Modern Art and Music," *Renaissance Studies* 28, no. 1 (2014): 50–70.).

his unimpressive presence (2 Cor 10:10), which may not be primarily about his physical appearance. Ancient physiognomics saw the correlation between physical appearance and bodily impulses,[16] which, by implication, reflected the person's character and ability. While the Scripture does not deny that society's favor often rests on a person's physical characteristics (e.g. Luke 2:52; 19:3), this is not what the Scripture underscores (1 Sam 16:7).

Roman Citizen

The NT does not provide detailed information about Paul's physical stature, but it does provide some information about his social stature. First, Paul claimed to be a Roman citizen. This makes Paul a Jew by race but one who was both influenced by the ancient Greek culture and a citizen of Rome in terms of his political identity.[17] It is possible that Paul was a descendant of a freedman who had acquired citizenship[18] and, as such, Paul was able to claim that he was a citizen by birth (Acts 22:28).

While Paul and Silas were preaching the gospel in Philippi, they performed an exorcism on a clairvoyant slave girl. This angered her masters because they lost income after the slave girl lost her ability to tell fortunes. The slave owners brought their complaint to the magistrates, accusing Paul and Silas as Jews of causing disturbance to the city introducing customs unlawful and unacceptable for the Romans (Acts 16:20–21). This complaint led to their imprisonment. The Roman authorities responded impulsively to the crowd's outcry, publicly beating and imprisoning Paul and Silas without a fair trial (16:22–23). They were not proven guilty of any crime so the magistrates, eventually, attempted to release them quietly so that it would appear as if nothing unlawful had happened (16:36). It should be noted that Paul asserted his rights as a citizen, not to argue the legality of his preaching nor to defend his religious liberty to do

---

16. Abraham J. Malherbe, "A Physical Description of Paul," *Harvard Theological Review* 79, no. 1 (1986): 171. See also Pseudo Aristotle, *Physiognomonics* 805a.

17. There are some who question the historicity of Paul's claim to be a Roman citizen (e.g. W. Stegemann, "War der Paulus ein römischer Bürger?," *Zeitschrift für die neutestamentliche Wissenschaft und die Kunde der älteren Kirche* 78 (1987): 200–29. However, many Pauline scholars see no reason to reject Paul's claim (see F. F. Bruce, *Paul: Apostle of the Free Spirit* [Exeter: Paternoster Press, 1977]; Colin J. Hemer, *The Book of Acts in the Setting of Hellenistic History*, Wissenschaftliche Untersuchungen zum Neuen Testament 49 [Tübingen: Mohr Siebeck, 1989]).

18. Peter van Minnen, "Paul the Roman Citizen," *Journal for the Study of the New Testament* 17, no. 56 (1995): 43–52. Legally born Romans were registered in their hometown's public records, and the letters *c.r.e.* (*civem romanum esse* or "he is a Roman") were inscribed on their birth certificates as proofs of their citizenship. See Eckhard J. Schnabel, *Acts*, Zondervan Exegetical Commentary on the New Testament (Grand Rapids: Zondervan, 2012), 687.

so; instead, he asserted his rights to be protected from police brutality.[19] This incident gives us a glimpse of the legal and penal systems of the first-century Roman Empire. Paul's refusal to quietly leave shows that there were privileges Roman citizens enjoyed (16:37–40).[20] Such privileges included: voting; freedom from degrading forms of punishment, which Paul was asserting in this incident; and the right to appeal to Rome, which Paul did after his trial made no progress for two years under the corrupt proconsul, Felix (24:26–27), and had to restart with another proconsul, Festus (25:10–12; 26:32).[21] Presumably, these were privileges that were not granted to non-citizens.

Paul's appeal to his Roman citizenship while imprisoned in the Philippian jail was not the last record in Acts of such an incident.[22] After being arrested in Jerusalem and being mistaken as the Egyptian leader of four thousand insurrectionists and assassins (21:37–38; compare Josephus, *Jewish Antiquities* 20.9.6 §§167–72; *Jewish Wars* 2.13.5 §§261–63), Paul spoke before the Roman tribune and also informed them that he was a Roman citizen. In both Philippi (Macedonia) and Caesarea, Paul appealed to his Roman citizenship to assert his rights for protection from unlawful punishments. Again, the reason for his appeal was that some Roman authorities abused their power and he was tortured even without being proven guilty (Acts 22:25–26). The tribune responded to Paul's claim that he, too, was a Roman citizen whose citizenship had been bought, to which Paul responded by saying that he was born with the privilege (22:27–29). This conversation suggests that there were various ways to obtain Roman citizenship during the time of Paul, and the way the conversation went hints to the prevalent corruption in those days in relation to obtaining citizenship – some were able to purchase their citizenship, giving them a better standing in society and better opportunities.[23]

---

19. Boyd Reese, "Apostle Paul's Exercise of His Rights as a Roman Citizen as Recorded in the Book of Acts," *Evangelical Quarterly* 47 (1975): 142.

20. Everett Ferguson, *Backgrounds of Early Christianity*, 3rd ed. (Grand Rapids: Eerdmans, 2003), 63.

21. For a more detailed discussion on the identity of Sergius Paulus, see F. J. Foakes-Jackson and Kirsopp Lake, *The Beginnings of Christianity*, 5 vols. (London: Macmillan, 1933), 5:464–74.

22. Brian Rapske cautions about overestimating the value of Paul's Roman citizenship in regard to his trial. For sure, citizenship brings advantages, but the "un-Roman" timing of his revelation of his citizenship may also raise some question about its value. See *Paul in Roman Custody*, The Book of Acts in First Century Setting 3 (Grand Rapids: Eerdmans, 1994), 72.

23. Purchasing citizenship was clearly not the normal way of obtaining it. Ferguson lists the following as methods to obtain Roman citizenship: birth to citizen parents, manumission of slaves of citizens at Rome, as a special favor for services rendered to the empire, and being part of auxiliary forces (see *Backgrounds of Early Christianity*, 62–63).

Jewish and Hellenistic Education

Being uprooted and dispersed had been part of the Jewish identity, especially for those in the diaspora. After the exile, the Jews responded to this fact either by aiming for their "return" or by redefining themselves as the "people of the Book."[24] In the case of Paul, he seemed to have tried to achieve both by studying in Jerusalem and his constant visiting there, and also through his commitment to the study of the Torah.

Paul claimed to have been educated under a Pharisee, Gamaliel, who followed a strict system of teaching the law to his students (Acts 22:3; 26:5). As a Roman citizen, Paul could be considered part of the elite in Roman society; being a Pharisee potentially placed him among the elite in Jewish communities as well.[25] His education might attest to his family's social background.[26] Paul never mentioned his financial status in any of his letters, but in exhorting the Philippians about contentment, he mentioned that he personally experienced having plenty and having meager resources (Phil 4:12). In this context, while he was clearly grateful for the generosity of the Macedonians toward him so that he could experience abundance, it is also possible that he was referring to his family of origin. Being a Roman citizen may also suggest that he came from a family that had substantial wealth.[27] In addition, paying for his education suggests that Paul might have belonged to a family that, at the very least, enjoyed some kind of financial stability sufficient to pay for his education.

One of the difficulties of receiving education in diaspora is learning cultural values and acquiring habits and practices that are different from that of one's ethnic origin. For instance, this is one of the struggles of Asian-Americans, even those who belong to the third generation.[28] Receiving a foreign education may not necessarily be a bad thing, but when there are cultural

---

24. Gruen, *Diaspora*, 232.

25. Ben Witherington III, *The Paul Quest: The Renewed Search for the Jew of Tarsus* (Downers Grove: InterVarsity Press, 1998), 94.

26. Gerd Theissen suggests that Paul might have belonged to an upper-class family in Tarsus. As a tentmaker, he was part of a guild that did not enjoy an honorable social position (see Dio Chrysostom, *Second Tarsic Discourse* 34.21–23) but the fact that his family was able to secure citizenship of Tarsus and Rome suggests that his family had enjoyed a degree of prominence. See Gerd Theissen, *The Social Setting of Pauline Christianity: Essays on Corinth*, ed. and trans. John H. Schültz (Philadelphia: Fortress, 1982), 104–5. Enjoying prominence and financial means is different from using them to "purchase" citizenship (cf. Acts 22:28).

27. William M. Ramsay, *St. Paul the Traveller and Roman Citizen* (New York: Putnam's Sons, 1898), 31.

28. Julius-Kei Kato, *How Immigrant Christians Living in Mixed Cultures Interpret Their Religion: Asian-American Diasporic Hybridity and Its Implication for Hermeneutics* (Lewiston: Edwin Mellen Press, 2012), 85.

values that contradict one's own, it is challenging. We can expect Paul to have experienced the same struggles as he was being educated in Tarsus. Whether it was his own or his family's motivation to study the Torah, a Jewish education was a necessity, more than a luxury.

Josephus wrote that the Jewish law required Jews to educate their children with the law and to teach them the deeds of their forefathers so as to imitate their good deeds (Josephus, *Against Apion* 2.26 §204).[29] This form of education must begin, as Josephus also noted, in infancy (cf. Deut 6:1–2). Paul must have received this form of home education as well. His claim of being "circumcised on the eighth day" (Phil 3:5) reveals not so much about Paul and his own religiosity but about his parents and their faithfulness to the law because no eight-day-old baby can go to the priest by himself to be circumcised. It is highly likely that the same religious parents who brought him to the priest for circumcision also taught him the law as a child.

Paul did not only receive informal education at home typical of a Jewish household; he went through formal Jewish training and was mentored by Gamaliel. The collection of Mishnah allows us a peek into the inchoate form of rabbinic training, with different teachers proffering their interpretations of the Jewish law. This shows us that an important element in their training was interpreting Scripture. Paul's letters include citations and allusions to passages from the Old Testament (OT), including brief expositions of them. Aside from references to the Jewish Scripture, he also showed familiarity with the works of some Greek philosophers, which suggests that Paul might have also received formal Greek education even though he did not explicitly claim it. In his brief self-introduction before the magistrates in Caesarea, Paul mentioned that he was from Tarsus, alongside his training under Gamaliel (Acts 22:3). By mentioning Tarsus together with his Pharisaic training, Paul could have been hinting at his Greek education. Tarsus, Athens, and Alexandria were the three ancient cities within the Roman Empire known as centers for Greek education in their respective regions. Strabo described Tarsus and its residents this way

> The people at Tarsus have devoted themselves so eagerly, not only to philosophy, but also to the whole round of education in general, that they have surpassed Athens, Alexandria, or any other place

---

29. Narry F. Santos underscores the importance of modelling and intergenerational mission as exemplified by Jesus among the Jews in Judea and also by Paul among the Christian communities, which include both dispersed Jews and native Gentiles. See his "Intergenerational Mission in the New Testament: Examples of Life-on-Life Modeling by Jesus and Paul," in *From Womb to Tomb: Generational Missiology in the 21st Century and Beyond*, ed. Sadiri Joy Tira (Edmonton: Pagemaster Publishing, 2024), 62–63.

that can be named where there have been schools and lectures of philosophers. But it is so different from other cities that there the men who are fond of learning are all natives, and foreigners are not inclined to sojourn there; neither do these natives stay there, but they complete their education abroad; and when they have completed it they are pleased to live abroad, and but few go back home. But the opposite is the case with the other cities which I have just mentioned except Alexandria; for many resort to them and pass time there with pleasure, but you would not see many of the natives either resorting to places outside their country through love of learning or eager about pursuing learning at home. With the Alexandrians, however, both things take place, for they admit many foreigners and also send not a few of their own citizens abroad. Further, the city of Tarsus has all kinds of schools of rhetoric; and in general it not only has a flourishing population but also is most powerful, thus keeping up the reputation of the mother-city. (Strabo, *Geography* 14.5.13)[30]

Paul grew up in such an environment. However, the evaluation of many patristic writers of Paul's ability to write and communicate was not always friendly and positive. John Chrysostom criticized Paul's eloquence, saying that Paul "did not display powerful eloquence ... unlearned, to the lowest degree of poor learning" (*De laudibus sancti Pauli apostoli* 4.10).[31] Augustine uses Romans 5:3–5 to point to Paul's "incompetence" in grammar and rhetoric (*Christian Doctrine* 4.7.11).[32] Likewise, Irenaeus noted Paul's unconventional syntax in 2 Corinthians and other letters (*Against Heresies* 3.7.1–2).[33] The patristic writers, for sure, were more adept in Koine Greek (the variation of the ancient Greek language used by Paul and later by the church fathers) than anyone from the generations after them, since they used the same language Paul used. It should be noted that Paul never claimed to have superior writing and oratorical skills. On the contrary, Paul on occasions disparaged his own

---

30. Based on the translation of Horace Leonard Jones of the Loeb Classical Library.

31. Margaret M. Mitchell, *John Chrysostom on Paul: Praises and Problem Passages*, Writings from the Greco-Roman World 48 (Atlanta: SBL Press, 2022), 745.

32. Based on Timothy George, *Augustine: On Christian Doctrine and Selected Introductory Works*, Theological Foundations (Nashville: B&H Academic, 2022).

33. Based on *The Ante-Nicene Fathers*, Alexander Roberts and James Donaldson, eds., vol. 1 (Peabody: Hendrickson, 1885–1887). For comments of other church fathers, see Ryan S. Schellenberg, "Τὸ εν λόγω ιδιωτικὸν τοῦ Ἀποστόλου: Revisiting Patristic Testimony on Paul's Rhetorical Education," *Novum Testamentum* 54, no. 4 (2012): 359–63.

skills in communication (1 Cor 1:17; 2 Cor 11:6); he was also criticized by some of his contemporaries for his communication skills (2 Cor 10:10). There is really no need to idealize him; as he himself claimed, he preferred to glory in his weaknesses (1 Cor 2:3; 2 Cor 11:30; 12:5, 9) because it is through weaknesses that God's glory is seen clearly. One must remember that there is a huge space between incompetence and sagacity. Paul's skill might not have gained the approval of some patristic writers in terms of his writing ability; however, there is no question that it was through him and his ministry that the gospel was proclaimed in a number of European regions, and it was he who penned thirteen of the twenty-seven writings we now call the New Testament – the authority of which the patristics also recognized.

Ramsay describes Paul this way

> [T]he Paul of Acts is the Paul that appears to us in his own letters, in his ways and his thoughts, in his educated tone of polished courtesy, in his quick and vehement temper, in the extraordinary versatility and adaptability which made him at home in every society, moving at ease in all surroundings, and everywhere the centre of interest, whether he is the Socratic dialectician in the agora of Athens, or the rhetorician in its University, or conversing with kings and proconsuls, or advising in the council on shipboard, or cheering a broken-spirited crew to make one more effort for life. Wherever Paul is, no one present has eyes for any but him.[34]

Ethnicity and Religion

Ethnicity and religion are two different things, and while a person's ethnic background and religious views are not always tied together, in the case of the Jews, the two have a close relationship. Their religious identity is based on the nation's history with Israel being set apart to serve God.

The short autobiographical section of Paul's letter to the Philippians provides information about his religious credentials, which includes his upbringing, affiliation, and practice. Paul was a Jew by birth, and not a proselyte.[35] It was briefly discussed earlier that having been circumcised on the eighth day (Phil 3:5) does not say much about Paul's personal devotion though it does

---

34. Ramsay, *Paul the Traveller*, 21–22.
35. Roji Thomas George, *Philippians: A Pastoral and Contextual Commentary*, Asia Bible Commentary Series (Carlisle: Langham Global Library, 2019), 111.

inform about his religious upbringing. He could have been circumcised only because his parents or guardians brought him for circumcision on the exact day prescribed by the law (Lev 12:3; cf. Gen 17:12). This physical mark is one of God's requirements from his people (Gen 17:14) and, having met that requirement, Paul could boldly claim that he was "of the people of God" (see Phil 3:5), as the OT defines it.

Ethnic groups are often identified by certain physical markers. Ancient Ishmaelites, for instance, were identified by wearing gold earrings (Judg 8:24). Even at present, physical markers like clothes, hairstyle, and posture are used to distinguish one ethnic group from another, such as the ethnic groups in Madagascar.[36] In their case, there are no ethnic conflicts, rather, these ethnic markers help each group identify the people with whom they can cooperate in certain circumstances. In the case of the ancient Jews, the physical marker was circumcision.

This was not always seen positively, however, especially after the second century BC when some young Jewish men adopted the Hellenistic practice of exercising nude in gymnasia and underwent epispasm, a surgical procedure to reverse their circumcision.[37] Removing one's ethnic identity marker signifies, at the very least, a conscious dissociation from certain aspects of one's cultural origin. One example is the cutting of the queue (pigtail) by some diasporan Chinese in the Philippines during the Spanish era because the hairstyle was associated with their subjugation by Manchu rulers of the Qing Dynasty.[38] In the case of the young Jewish men in the diaspora, epispasm was their attempt to gain acceptability among the uncircumcised. Paul disapproved of this practice (1 Cor 7:18), not because he refused to identify with the Greeks but because he considered it glorious to be a circumcised Jew, as one having the physical mark of the members of the OT "people of God."

In addition, Paul traced his ancestry back to the tribe of Benjamin.[39] By the first century AD, the tribe of Benjamin no longer enjoyed the prominence it once had after it produced the first king of Israel (1 Sam 9:1–2; 10:1). The tribe

---

36. Bram Tucker, et al. "Ethnic Markers Without Ethnic Conflict: Why Do Interdependent Masikoro, Mieka, And Vezo of Madagascar Signal Their Ethnic Differences?," *Human Nature* 32, no. 3 (2021): 529–56.

37. See 1 Maccabees 1:15; Josephus, *Jewish Antiquities* 12.5.1 §241; Paul A. Holloway, *Philippians*, ed. Adela Yarbro Collins (Minneapolis: Fortress, 2017), 157.

38. Uytanlet, *Hybrid Tsinoys*, 43.

39. Gerald F. Hawthorne listed several reasons why someone would consider it honorable to be part of the tribe of Benjamin. See Gerald F. Hawthorne, *Philippians*, Word Biblical Commentary 43 (Waco: Word Books, 1983), 132–33.

of Benjamin was apportioned lands contiguous to those of Judah (Josh 18:21–28) and, when the kingdom was divided, the tribe was eventually absorbed by Judah (1 Kgs 12:21), making the Benjamites "Jews," not because they descended from Judah but because they were residents of Judea. The claim to "purity" of race was underscored by Paul's assertion of being a Hebrew of Hebrews (Phil 3:5). This expression may refer to his fluency in the Hebrew language (Acts 21:40; 22:2; 26:14; cf. 6:1), as well as to his status as a descendant of Abraham, the first Hebrew (Gen 14:13). Abraham had many biological children, but not all of them belong to God's people. To be a Hebrew of Hebrews may mean that Paul claimed to belong to an elite group among Abraham's children. George summarizes the significance of Paul's claim to racial purity as follows.

> Within the first-century Palestinian nationalistic context, Hebrew identity signified ethnic purity. Unlike Hellenized Jews, who compromised Jewish cultural purity to thrive in the Hellenistic world, those contending for Jewish cultural essentialism (as during the Maccabean revolt) resisted cultural mixture for political reasons (1 Macc 2). In other words, the claim is not merely for the purity of blood, a "blue-blooded" Jew, but is also a certification for his faithful adherence to cultural purity despite being born and brought up outside of Palestine (Acts 21:39). In other words, his diasporic upbringing has not diluted his pure Jewishness.[40]

Racial purity is one interpretation of the expression "Hebrew of Hebrews." Another interpretation highlights the many ways in which Paul crossed boundaries. The term "Hebrew" is from the expression *ha ivri*, "the one who crossed over" (a river or boundary) – first used for describing Abraham's life as a sojourner. Paul traced his lineage back to a people who lived a nomadic lifestyle, who moved from Canaan to Egypt, from there crossed over the Red Sea to the wilderness, crossed over the Jordan River to the promised land, crossed over national boundaries to Babylonian exile, and in the case of Paul's family, eventually ended up in Tarsus. As a Hebrew of Hebrews, he crossed a lot of national boundaries. As a missionary, he also crossed multiple cultural boundaries.

Paul amplified his claim to religious devotion by mentioning his involvement in the Pharisaic movement. The Pharisees had a history of involvement

---

40. George, *Philippians*, 112. Moisés Silva also considers the expression "Hebrew of Hebrews" as having a "climactic intent" to stress that Paul is "pure blooded" and his "denial that he had any mixed ancestry." See his *Philippians*, Baker Exegetical Commentary on the New Testament (Grand Rapids: Baker, 1992), 176.

in local politics (e.g. Mark 3:6; 8:15; 12:13) and religious proselytizing (e.g. Matt 23:15), but the one aspect of the movement that Paul highlighted was its commitment to the law (Phil 3:5). The group had the reputation of being interpreters of the law. The rift between Jesus and the Pharisees partly focused on legal interpretations (e.g. Matt 5:21–48). The Pharisees are often presented negatively in the Gospels because of their participation in the death of Jesus and their proclivity toward maintaining only a proper religious image. However, this negative portrayal should not erase the fact that, as a movement, their commitment to the interpretation of Scripture was unquestionable. As an interpreter of the law, Paul was committed to the study, practice, and teaching of the law (Ezra 7:10). On the one hand, this commitment was good because it made the devotee fully dedicated to God, thus Paul could claim to have been blameless in following the law (Phil 3:6). On the other hand, this commitment, if unchecked, could lead to the kind of religious extremism about which Jesus warned his disciples (John 16:2–3) and to which Paul readily admitted having lived (Phil 3:6).

Paul's enthusiasm should not be construed as an association with the liberation movements or bandits of his time, despite the fact that individuals in these groups were also characterized by their zeal. It can be understood in the light of Phinehas's zeal for obeying the law (Num 25:7–13; Ps 106:30) and intolerance of those that showed lack of commitment to follow the law's requirements. Torrey Seland describes the zealots this way: "early zealots probably did not form any consistent party or movement, but were vigilant individuals who took the law in their own hands when observing cases of gross Torah transgressions."[41] Zeal is a praiseworthy quality as seen also in the works of Philo. For instance, he commended Phinehas even for being violent because it was done out of zeal (*Special Laws* 1.9.54–10.57).[42] Zeal was considered a religious duty,[43] thus it is not surprising that Paul and many of his contemporaries resorted to violence in dealing with Christians. This kind of response is one that Jesus never advocated; indeed, he had spoken against it (e.g. Luke 22:49–53).

There is no denying that despite being in the diaspora, with all the struggles that come with it, Paul found an environment where he could thrive. As Ben Witherington summarizes,

---

41. Torrey Seland, "Saul of Tarsus and Early Zealotism Reading Gal 1:13–14 in Light of Philo's Writings," *Biblica* 83, no. 4 (2002): 449–50.

42. Materials from Philo's works are based on the translation of C. D. Yonge, *The Works of Philo: Complete and Unabridged*, New Updated Version (Peabody: Hendrickson, 1993).

43. For a more comprehensive discussion of Philo's understanding of zealotry, see Seland, "Saul of Tarsus and Early Zealotism," 456–62.

> When we think of the social portrait of Paul in Acts, we think of Paul the man of the world equally at home with Jews and Gentiles, with those of low and high social status, with men and women. We think of an educated Paul capable of considerable rhetorical skill as reflected in his speeches, and a Paul who knows at least basic Greek philosophy and Jewish belief and practice in detail. He is at once a loyal Jew, a loyal Christian, a good Roman citizen, and apparently a citizen of Tarsus ("no mean city"). We think of a Paul who works miracles and works with his hands, and a Paul who itinerates throughout the eastern half of the Mediterranean. He is at once evangelist and teacher, pastor and preacher, deeply loved and greatly hated.[44]

Paul continued to thrive as a Jewish missionary in diaspora, but the struggles, rejections, and persecution intensified as we shall see in the succeeding discussions. This Jew who was at-home in the diaspora would eventually become unhomed.

A Home for a Credentialled Diasporan Jew

One adjective describes Paul's credentials: impressive! A religious family upbringing and one that very likely belonged to an honorable class; a citizenship to which many of his contemporaries could only have aspired; education that most of the population could not have imagined; skills in a trade that allowed him to be independent; opportunities to travel to various regions that gave him a broader perspective of the world; proficiency in more than one language that allowed him to communicate with Jews and Gentiles alike, with religious people and philosophers, and with people from all walks of life; a religious zeal that gave him a good standing, especially with the religious Jews; and a religious affiliation that allowed him to rub elbows with the influential people and groups in society. Paul was at-home wherever he went. This changed as he transitioned from being a zealous Pharisee to a follower of Jesus committed to bringing the message of the gospel to the ends of the earth. Paul had credentials that looked good on paper until he met the resurrected Christ!

---

44. Ben Witherington III, *The Acts of the Apostles: A Socio-Rhetorical Commentary* (Grand Rapids: Eerdmans, 1998), 432.

3

Unhomed Follower of the Way

Despite modern sensitivities on religious freedom and mutual respect, religious violence continues in many parts of the world, including Asia. Nicholas F. Gier proposes, "Whenever religious and national identities are fused, one will find religiously motivated violence."[1] This is not only true in modern religious settings.[2] The same was true about ancient Jews and how they related to Jewish believers of Jesus.

Religious zeal was something many ancient Jews would have considered a commendable quality worth pursuing, as discussed in the previous chapter. Such zeal, when taken to the extreme, still leads zealous people to commit horrendous acts against those they perceive as unfaithful or undevoted. This unrestrained zeal is at the root of much religious violence. Paul himself admitted to having participated in such violence (Phil 3:6); he also later realized that, in Christ, what was supposedly a "gain" was actually rubbish (3:7). Then, as now, "gain" could be in the form of a pristine *image* of faith and devotion that can affect other people's reputation, future, opportunities, properties, and even lives.

In this chapter, we will go through Paul's journey from being a persecutor to being one of the persecuted. As a persecutor, he was at-home among the Jewish religious authorities who displaced the followers of Jesus and caused them to become unhomed. After his encounter with Christ, he remained faith-

---

1. Nicholas F. Gier, *The Origins of Religious Violence: An Asian Perspective* (Lanham: Lexington Books, 2014), 252. In this work, Gier discusses the kind of religious violence happening in various parts of Asia, including the Mongols and Muslims in India, Buddhists in Sri Lanka and Burma, and Christians in China, among others.

2. Religious nationalism is also discussed in relation to submission to authority with those in power who require blind submission and the tension this creates among those who call for justice and truth. See Jesudas M. Athyal, "Church and Nationalism," *South Asia Bible Commentary*, ed. Brian Wintle, et al. (Rajasthan: Open Door Publications, 2015), 1545.

ful to Judaism as many of the Jewish believers were. He experienced both being unhomed among the believers because of his violent treatment of them in the past and being at-home with them because believers such as Ananias and Barnabas vouched for him. His journey continued to the point that he had conflict with the unbelieving Jews, the group to which he was formerly affiliated, causing him to be unhomed among them.

At-Home with the Jerusalem Authorities, Displacing the Followers of the Way

The first recorded account of persecution in Acts is the incident involving the religious authorities and the two apostles, Peter and John. The priests and the Sadducees tried to silence Peter and John for preaching about Jesus and his resurrection (Acts 4:8–18). The issue was partly theological and doctrinal because the priests and the Sadducees did not believe in the resurrection (23:6–8). There are inevitably elements of power and benefaction in this account, except that the benefaction did not come in the form of finances, for which the lame man originally begged, but in the form of "servant-benefaction," which pointed the beneficiary to the divine savior.[3] Keeping the people from believing the teachings of the apostles was difficult, especially as they were backed by healings and miraculous acts, which the religious leaders also admitted (4:16). Observing the impact of these "uneducated, common men" (4:13) and witnessing the people's growing belief in the apostles (4:14–16), the priests, motivated by their religious zeal, used their power to arrest and imprison the apostles (4:17–18).

This opposition against the followers of Jesus continues in the following chapters of Acts, bringing us to the story of Stephen's death. Stephen did not explicitly preach about the resurrection of Jesus, although this is implied in his vision of Jesus as "the Son of Man standing at the right hand of God" (7:56) and his message regarding the destruction and rebuilding of the temple (6:14). The point of contention the religious leaders raised against Stephen was that he spoke blasphemous words against Moses, against God, and against the temple, and that he proclaimed that Jesus would destroy the temple and change the customs handed down by Moses (6:11–14). While the religious authorities called false witnesses to speak against Stephen (6:13), this does not mean that their lies were not partially based on facts. This was the same issue hurled against Jesus (Matt 27:40; Mark 14:58), because Jesus indeed used the destruction and

---

3. Craig S. Keener, *Acts: An Exegetical Commentary*, 4 vols. (Grand Rapids: Baker Academic, 2012–2015), 2:1147.

rebuilding of the temple as a metaphor for his death and resurrection (John 2:19), and Stephen might have preached the same message. The witnesses called by the religious authorities were false because they misappropriated Stephen's message and testified maliciously to have him put to death. Their testimonies were coated with some facts to give an impression of reliability.

There is nothing in the early part of Stephen's speech with which the religious leaders would have disagreed, even his comments about the temple (Acts 7:48-49), because he simply reviewed Jewish history (7:1-47). Stephen's claim that no physical structure could house the Lord (7:49) might not have been something that the religious authorities would have disagreed with because this is clear even in the OT (2 Sam 7:5-6). Although God honored David's desire to build a house for God to dwell in (1 Kgs 6:11-13; 2 Chr 6:2), the temple was the physical symbol of God's presence with his people and it was, at times, referred to as God's dwelling place (2 Chr 36:15). Any devout Jew would have known that God cannot be confined within a physical structure (1 Kgs 8:27, 30, 39, 43, 49; 2 Chr 6:18, 21, 30, 33, 39). Stephen's final words made it clear that the religious authorities were angered because he called them out for their disobedience (Acts 7:50-53). Luke described the aftermath of Stephen's speech as "when they heard these things they were enraged, and they ground their teeth at him" (7:54).

Prior to his death, Stephen declared his heavenly vision of Jesus standing at the right hand of God (7:56). At this, those who had earlier ground their teeth in anger (7:54) covered their ears (7:57). The covering of one's ears could be considered an act of piety in response to what was perceived as blasphemous words. It was done to prevent blasphemies from entering the ears of the pious to afflict their souls (Philo, *Decalogue* 13.63).[4]

Stephen was immediately taken out of the city to be executed as prescribed in the OT (Lev 24:16; Num 15:35; see also Mishnah, Sanhedrin 6:1). While the less essential details, such as the venue for execution, were upheld, the other more essential procedural elements of a trial seem to have been neglected. One has to ask how Stephen was executed without the approval of the Romans. F. F. Bruce suggests that Stephen's offence of speaking against the temple could be categorized under "offence against the temple for which the Roman administration, as an exceptional concession, allowed the Jewish authorities to carry out the death sentence without reference to the governor."[5] Even if this was the

---

4. Schnabel, *Acts*, 390.

5. F. F. Bruce, *The Book of Acts*, The New International Commentary on the New Testament, rev. ed. (Grand Rapids: Eerdmans, 1988), 159.

case, it still does not explain why the religious authorities were adamant that the execution was done immediately. Their adamance was physically apparent, as Luke noted, in the gnashing of their teeth (Acts 7:54).

The Mishnah provides a glimpse of the legal procedure that was to be followed by the Sanhedrin, from the composition of the court (Mishnah Sanhedrin 1:1–6), to the roles of the priests and kings (2:1–8), to the procedure in choosing judges and witnesses (3:1–5), to the procedure on how judges were to interrogate witnesses (3:6–4:2). In capital cases, the process was more tedious with a longer interrogation period (5:1–2). If there were no sufficient reasons to sentence the accused, the *acquittal was to be immediate* but if the evidence pointed to culpability, the likely *guilty verdict required delay*. If there was disagreement among the members of the court, they were to seek additional opinion; they could not sentence a person to death just because the majority said so (5:5). Even on the day of execution, with new evidence (6:1) or with a confession (6:2), the sentence for guilt could still have been reversed. Bruce aptly summarizes the law's hesitance to execute a person, "In the Mishnah this (or any other) form of execution is treated as an unwelcome necessity, to be avoided if the slightest legal loophole can be found; Luke does not give the impression that Stephen's executioners stoned him reluctantly as a disagreeable but unavoidable duty."[6]

The religious leaders' adamance resulted in Stephen's *swift* execution. This is the story where Paul first appeared in Luke's account (Acts 7:58). Paul might not have directly participated in the stoning but, as the guardian of the executioners' garments, his involvement in Stephen's death was clear. The principle is similar to that of David's baggage guardians who shared in as much spoil and honor as those who went to the battle (2 Sam 25:13; 30:24). Paul shared as much "honor" (more precisely, "guilt") as those who took stones to throw at Stephen. The reason the executioners stripped themselves might have been for convenience, so that their garments would not hinder their physical movements as they threw stones. Luke did not mention whether Stephen's clothes were removed before he was stoned. Ironically, the legal requirements included stripping the guilty party (the one to be stoned) of clothing[7] but, in this instance, the executioners were the ones stripped of clothing – as if they were the ones who were actually guilty.

Luke explicitly mentioned that after the stoning Paul "approved of [Stephen's] execution" (Acts 8:1). Such approval was tantamount to saying that

---

6. Bruce, *The Book of Acts*, 160.
7. Mishnah, Sanhedrin 6:3.

Paul was a participant in the murder of the prophets, a charge Jesus raised in his exchange of words with the lawyers (Luke 11:48).[8] Paul did not remain a passive participant in attacking the church; after this time, he was the head of the pack as he began "ravaging the church, and entering house after house, he dragged off men and women and committed them to prison" (Acts 8:3). The Greek word *lumainō*, translated in the ESV as "ravaging," can refer to both physical and mental ill-treatment.[9] The psychological torture cannot be separated from the physical violence done against the followers of Christ at this time, especially given this organized attack instigated by this zealous Pharisee. The Jewish believers in Jerusalem would have been always on the lookout because they could have been next.

Even as a young Pharisee, Paul must have been well-connected and enjoyed much support from the religious authorities otherwise he would not have been able to spearhead such violent acts, including imprisoning the believers. Luke's account verifies Paul's claim that he was advancing in Judaism way beyond his contemporaries. His loyalty to his religion and commitment to the tradition of his ancestors motivated him to persecute the church and, as he admitted, he "persecuted the church of God *violently* and tried to destroy it" (Gal 1:13–14, italics mine). Paul was so *at-home in Judaism* that his actions caused the *believers to be unhomed* and displaced. In the NT, the word *diaspeirō* ("disperse") is only used three times, and all of them refer to the displacement of believers as a result of persecution initiated by Paul (Acts 8:1, 4; cf. 11:19). In contrast to the dispersed Jews in the OT, the followers of Christ in Acts were dispersed, not because of their unfaithfulness to God but because of their faithfulness to Christ.

At-Home with the Jewish Authorities, Unhomed Jewish Followers of the Way in Jerusalem

The dispersion of the believers in Jerusalem did not satisfy Paul. Luke noted the positive outcome of the dispersion in that those who were scattered began proclaiming Christ wherever they went (Acts 8:4–5). Paul's zeal clearly led him to try to silence both the believers in Jerusalem and those who were scattered

---

8. Keener, *Acts*, 2:1463.

9. C. K. Barrett suggests that, in this context, the ill-treatment is primarily physical. See *The Acts of the Apostles*, International Critical Commentary, 2 vols. (Edinburgh: T&T Clark, 1994), 1:393. Although one may ask whether the mental/psychological component can really be separable from the physical violence done.

abroad. He proactively pursued them, making sure that even the religious authorities were on board with his plan. Paul went to the high priest to ask for a letter to the synagogues of Damascus so he could arrest the believers in Syria (9:1–2).[10] This shows how methodical Paul was in trying to eliminate the followers of Jesus.

Luke narrated that the believers fled, but the apostles remained in Jerusalem. This may suggest, as Bruce succinctly concludes, "it was the Hellenists in the church (the group in which Stephen had been a leader) who formed the main target of attack, and that it was they for the most part who were compelled to leave Jerusalem."[11] This incident, along with the one about food distribution to widows (6:1–7), reflects the animosity between the Hebrew-speaking Jews and the Greek-speaking Jews. The tension was not racial but lingual – it was between two groups of the same ethnicity.[12] To some degree, the Greek-speakers were unhomed among the Hebrew speakers. Language differences can potentially cause tensions and communication problems, but this issue should not be detrimental to the health of the church. Having distinct groups within a community inevitably creates tensions and power struggles. Keener explains

> Luke undoubtedly has reasons for emphasizing that the apostles remained (other than employing them to symbolize the entire "Hebrew" faction). Perhaps Luke wishes to emphasize that they did not leave their posts; they were still contending for the soul of Jerusalem, from which they presumably rule (Luke 22:30; cf. 1:52). This could present the mother community as retaining (or seeking to retain) its sphere of authority over the believers spreading in the Diaspora; certainly, some leaders had to remain there for Jerusalem to remain the church's centre (even in Acts 12:17).[13]

The persecution of the Greek-speaking believers by the Jewish authorities does not mean that the believers who remained were safe. Peter and James later became targets of persecution, however that persecution was pursued by political authorities, not religious authorities (Acts 12:1–5). Paul's active participation in this atrocity displayed a sharp contrast between him and his teacher, Gamaliel. The record in Acts 5:34–39 portrays Gamaliel as a level-

---

10. The fact that Paul was able to make such a request also attests to his political credentials. See Rapske, *Paul in Roman Custody*, 100.

11. Bruce, *The Book of Acts*, 162; see also Keener, *Acts*, 2:1467–68.

12. For a brief discussion on the identity of these Hellenists, see Witherington, *Acts*, 240–47.

13. Keener, *Acts*, 2:1469. In addition, the courage of the apostles and the fact that diasporan churches were established by the bilingual groups are also underscored in the story.

headed leader who would not rush to take drastic action, especially if it meant causing harm to others, even those with whom he disagreed. The Paul we see in Acts 7–9 is one who could have benefitted from the advice of his mentor. Perhaps Gamaliel did advise Paul and the latter's zeal made him stubborn, or perhaps Gamaliel eventually changed his views about the matter and gave his blessings to Paul,[14] or perhaps he was totally unaware of Paul's plan.

Some early records show that Gamaliel had visited and been in touch with the governor in Syria to discuss some issues involving some bakers (Mishnah, Eduyot 7:7). This may suggest that Gamaliel had connections in Syria; if so, it is possible that Paul took advantage of these connections to advance his cause.[15] The right of extradition, first set during the time of Ptolemy VIII (1 Maccabees 15:21) and renewed later by Julius Caesar, might have still been in place, giving high priests the rights and privilege to take back lawbreakers who fled to Syria for refuge.[16] After Paul's persecution of the believers in Jerusalem, many believers were scattered throughout Judea and Samaria (Acts 8:1) and some sought refuge further north in Antioch of Syria (11:19). This means that when Paul requested a letter from the high priest, his primary target were the believers who were also refugees from Jerusalem who fled to Syria, and not those in Damascus. No wonder the disciples from Damascus, referring to those from Jerusalem, said that Paul went to Damascus "to bring *them* bound before the chief priest" (9:21, italics mine). Since these believers were Jews, they would have naturally sought refuge among the Jews. This explains Paul's request for a letter from the high priest to go to the synagogues in Damascus.

At-Home with the Jerusalem Authorities

An unusual thing happened while Paul was on his way to Damascus. He saw a bright light that blinded him (Acts 9:3, 8; 22:6; 26:13) and heard a voice from heaven (9:4; 22:7). The voice turned out to be that of Jesus, who asked why he was being persecuted (9:5; 22:8; 26:14). There were others who witnessed the incident: they saw the light (22:9), they heard the voice but saw no one speaking (9:7), and they did not understand what was said (22:9), maybe because the voice spoke in Hebrew (26:14). The voice told Paul to go to the city and

---

14. Schnabel, *Acts*, 395, 442. Joseph Klausner identifies the "impudent pupil of Gamaliel" (Babylonian Talmud, Shabbat 30b) with Paul. See his *From Jesus to Paul*, trans. William F. Stinespring (New York: Macmillan, 1943), 310–11.

15. Schnabel, *Acts*, 443.

16. Bruce, *The Book of Acts*, 180–81.

wait for further instructions (9:6) but revealed to him that he was appointed to be a witness who would proclaim the gospel to the Gentiles (26:16–18). This incident is sometimes referred to as Paul's "conversion," as one who changed religion from Judaism to Christianity.[17] One has to consider that Paul described this experience, not as a change of religion but as a calling to fulfil a vocation: "[God] who had set me apart before I was born, and who *called me by his grace*, was pleased to reveal his Son to me, in order that I might preach him among the Gentiles" (Gal 1:15–16, italics mine). Hans Dieter Betz correctly points out that

> One should not simply take for granted that Paul had a conversion experience in the sense that he was converted from Judaism to Christianity. At the time of his conversion the two religions were still one and the same, so that the most one could say is that he was converted from one Jewish movement, the Pharisees, to another, the Christians.[18]

Paul claimed to have been called from his mother's womb (Gal 1:5); this was comparable to Jeremiah's prophetic call (Jer 1:5). Paul described his new role as being "light to the Gentiles" (Acts 13:47), that is to "proclaim light both to our people and to the Gentiles" (26:23; cf. 9:15) and "to open their eyes, so that they may turn from darkness to light and from the power of Satan to God, that they may receive forgiveness of sins and a place among those who are sanctified by faith in [Christ]" (26:18). The task of being a light to the Gentiles (that is, the nations) was first given to the nation of Israel (Isa 42:6; 49:6), but history shows they were not able to complete it.

When Jesus was born Simeon announced that Jesus embodied God's salvation in that he was "a light for revelation to the Gentiles, and for glory to [God's] people Israel" (Luke 2:32). As the light to the nations, Jesus's task was to proclaim God's salvation to them. Similarly, Luke recorded Paul's speech wherein he claimed to share the same task as Jesus – being a light to the nations (both Jews and Gentiles) and proclaiming to them the message of God's salvation (Acts 13:47; 26:23). With Paul's new identity as a bearer of God's light, he began by proclaiming among the Jews in the synagogues of Damascus that Jesus is the Son of God (9:20). The changes in Paul's life were so drastic that the

---

17. Some define Paul's "conversion" as a "complete break from his past." Dieter Lührmann, *Galatians*, Continental Commentaries, trans. O. C. Dean, Jr. (Minneapolis: Fortress Press, 1992), 22. For a more nuanced definition of conversion, see Schnabel's discussion in his *Acts*, 458–61.

18. Hans Dieter Betz, *Galatians* (Philadelphia: Fortress Press, 1979), 69.

disciples at Damascus doubted that the change was real.[19] Luke described the situation this way, "And all who heard him were amazed and said, 'Is not this the man who made havoc in Jerusalem of those who called upon this name? And has he not come here for this purpose, to bring them bound before the chief priests?'" (9:21). There is no record that the Jewish authorities in Jerusalem were informed about what happened to Paul and, even if some of the Jewish leaders knew about the changes Paul experienced, there is no record that they immediately took action to silence Paul. The persecution against Paul would come later; thus, we may assume that for the time being Paul continued to enjoy good standing with the Jewish authorities in Jerusalem.

At-Home with the Disciples of Jesus, Unhomed Among the Unbelieving Jews in Damascus

The same cannot be said about the believers in Damascus, at least not initially. Paul's zeal for Judaism gave him an honorable standing among the Jewish authorities in Jerusalem, but his reputation as a persecutor of the believers preceded him in Damascus. In assessing what Paul did, the only adjective the Damascene believers could use to describe what Paul did to the believers in Jerusalem was "evil" (Acts 9:13). Although Jerusalem was where the apostles were based, Damascus was no less important because it had a large Jewish population and thus a significant number of synagogues[20] – and presumably a large number of believers. Their willingness or unwillingness to welcome Paul could have had either a beneficial or an adverse effect on Paul's ministry. It took an extraordinary incident, a divine revelation, to change the minds of the Damascene believers. The Lord revealed his plans for Paul to Ananias, one of the believers at Damascus (9:10–17). God told Ananias of Paul's role in the proclamation of the gospel to the Gentiles, the same gospel Ananias believed, and how Paul would suffer for the sake of God's name (9:15–16). Upon receiving the revelation, Ananias prayed for Paul's healing, baptized him, and provided refuge and hospitality for him among the believers in Damascus (9:18–19). By addressing Paul as "Brother Saul" (9:17), Ananias showed that

---

19. The presence of Jews in Damascus is well-attested. Josephus might have exaggerated the number in his account (e.g. *Jewish Wars* 7.6.6 §368), but the presence of Jews in the city need not be questioned. Moreover, considering that the presence of Damascene believers prior to Paul's arrival does not fit Luke's missionary scheme in Acts 1:8, there is no reason to doubt their presence there. See Keener, *Acts*, 2:1629–30.

20. Each synagogue was independent and had the freedom to self-supervise. See Bruce, *The Book of Acts*, 207.

he subsequently considered Paul as family by virtue of what we now refer to as "fictive kinship."[21] With the kindness and hospitality of Ananias, the former persecutor found a home among the disciples in Damascus. In other words, the transformation that occurred was not only in Paul. Ananias was also transformed from one who rejected the former persecutor to one who was hospitable to the future missionary.[22]

However, the safety Paul enjoyed was not guaranteed and did not last long. For some time, Paul took refuge among the Damascene believers as he continued preaching among the Jews in the synagogues (9:19–22). As Luke recounted, "When many days had passed, the Jews plotted to kill him" (9:23). With his proclamation of the gospel, Paul had made new enemies – the non-believers in Damascus. This means that even as Paul (presumably) continued to enjoy good standing with the Jewish authorities in Jerusalem and enjoyed being at-home among the Jewish believers in Damascus, he began to be unhomed among the non-believing Jews in Damascus such that they wanted him dead. This was the first recorded attempt at Paul's life after his encounter with the risen Lord, and it led Paul to flee to Jerusalem.

Unhomed Among the Unbelieving Hellenistic Jews, At-Home with the Followers of the Way in Jerusalem

The tables had turned. He who was once the persecutor had become the persecuted; the hunter had become the hunted. The kind of zeal that once led Paul to actively pursue the followers of Christ was apparently the same kind of zeal that made him a target of the Damascene Jews.[23] Luke described Paul's status thus, "Saul increased all the more in strength" (Acts 9:22), suggesting that his influence among the Jews in Damascus, both believers and non-believers, was increasing. With his intensifying influence, there was a growing target on his back. On the one hand, the dishonor Paul once experienced among the disciples in Damascus turned into honor because of the work he was doing (cf.

---

21. See David A. deSilva, *Honor, Patronage, Kinship & Purity: Unlocking New Testament Culture* (Downers Grove: InterVarsity Press, 2000), 199–231.

22. Noli P. Mendoza, "Faith at the Border, Faith on the Move: Migrations, Transitions, and Transformations in Acts 8–11," in *God at the Borders: Globalization, Migration and Diaspora*, ed. Charles R. Ringma, Karen Hollenbeck-Wuest, and Athena O. Gorospe (Mandaluyong: OMF Literature, 2005), 260–61.

23. It is important to note that there was no record of unbelieving Jews in Damascus persecuting the Damascene believers. It is possible that Paul's radical allies in Jerusalem sought to kill him and had plotted with the unbelieving Jews in Damascus. See Keener, *Acts*, 2:1674.

9:27). On the other hand, the honor he once enjoyed among the non-believing Jews for zealously protecting their traditions turned to dishonor – both for his proclamation that Jesus is the Christ and the confusion this proclamation caused among the Jews of Damascus (9:22).

Paul's increasing influence could only have meant one thing – that the power and influence of the non-believing Jews were decreasing.[24] Religious zeal and decreasing power or influence were a bad combination. In this situation, it seems that the solution the non-believing Jews opted for was Paul's elimination (9:23), but Paul escaped the Jews who plotted to kill him. Interestingly, instead of going back to his hometown of Tarsus, Paul went to Jerusalem to join the disciples there (9:26).

The respect the believers in Damascus had for Paul was not initially shared by the believers in Jerusalem, and for a legitimate reason. It took a divine revelation to Ananias (who was presumably advocating for Paul) before Paul was accepted into the community of Damascene believers (9:18–19). When Paul arrived at Jerusalem, he "attempted to join the disciples. And they were all afraid of him, for they did not believe that he was a disciple" (9:26). Aside from the gnawing memory of the harm that Paul inflicted upon the church, the believers had no immediate guarantee that Paul was not infiltrating them as some kind of undercover agent to cause them to break the law or to find reasons to arrest the members of the congregation.[25]

What Ananias did for Paul in Damascus, Barnabas did in Jerusalem. Barnabas argued on behalf of Paul based on the latter's track record in Damascus, albeit brief, as a herald for Christ (9:27). The disciples in Jerusalem feared associating with Paul because the last they had heard about Paul related to his treatment of the disciples in Jerusalem. Their hesitance is understandable. By the time Paul visited Jerusalem, "many days" had passed (9:23) and Paul had already been involved in mission (9:20). What the disciples of Jerusalem lacked was not information about Paul, but trust in him![26] Barnabas's basis for defending Paul was more than just humanitarian or compassion for an ostracized man. Barnabas defended Paul because there was a genuine sign of repentance

---

24. Luke only mentioned the opposition Paul faced against the unbelieving Jewish Damascenes, but Paul recalled the help provided to his persecutors by the Nabatean king, Aretas (2 Cor 11:32–33). Keener posits, "It would be politically savvy for a Nabatean ethnarch to accommodate Jewish concerns (or vice versa); if some of Jerusalem's official Jewish leadership approved the crackdown (as suggested in Acts 9:2), as Luke suggests, we might expect even further incentive to cooperate" (see Keener, *Acts*, 2:1675).

25. Bruce, *The Book of Acts*, 193.

26. Keener, *Acts*, 2:1689.

on the part of Paul, and his works also spoke on his behalf; Barnabas accepted the evidence that Paul was a changed man. With Barnabas's defense, the believers in Jerusalem accepted Paul into their community, and Paul became at-home with them (9:28). Paul did not disappoint them. With his acceptance into the community in Jerusalem, he began doing the same work, preaching "in the name of the Lord," speaking even to the Greek-speaking Jews (9:29).

With new friends, came new enemies. Luke's use of the description "Hellenists" to refer to those with whom Paul had disputes (9:29) may suggest both that the so-called "disciples" in Jerusalem (9:26) included both Hebrew-speaking and Greek-speaking followers of the Way (Acts 6) and that there were non-believing Greek-speaking Jews in Jerusalem who did not accept Paul's message. With the same zeal, these Hellenists, presumably members of the synagogue of the Freedman (6:9) from Paul's hometown in Cilicia,[27] also sought to kill Paul (9:29); and with this new threat, the believers thought it was best to send Paul back to Tarsus (9:30). Paul stayed in Tarsus until Barnabas went there to take him to Antioch (11:25).

Luke's silence about Paul's missionary activity in Tarsus is noteworthy. Paul's zeal in proclaiming the gospel message at this point in his life raises questions about why Luke mentioned nothing about Paul's ministry in his hometown yet there is a narration, albeit only in passing, concerning the return of Barnabas to Cyprus after he and Paul separated (15:39; cf. 13:4). Keener suggests that Paul did not get a good reception in his hometown.[28] If this is correct, Paul's reception reflected Jesus's earlier statement that "no prophet is acceptable in his hometown" (Luke 4:24; cf. John 4:44). As a zealous and well-educated diasporan Jew, and as a productive and law-abiding citizen of Rome, Paul's status in his hometown was well-received. As a missionary who was also a follower of Jesus, he was unhomed in his own hometown.

Religious Transition and Being Unhomed

According to Luke's accounts, in the period prior to Paul's receiving the call of Christ to ministry and in his first few years as a follower of Jesus, Paul encountered both believing Jews and non-believing Jews, Jews who were zealous for the law and those that were not, Jews from Jerusalem and those who were from the diaspora, those whose native language was Hebrew and those who were more Hellenized, and those with whom he was at-home and those with

---

27. Witherington, *Acts*, 325.
28. Keener, *Acts*, 2:1694.

whom he was unhomed. There may have been clear distinctions in terms of their commitment to Christ, their attitudes toward the law, their residences, languages, and their attitudes toward Paul, but there was no direct correlation between any two of these categories. This means that some who were devoted to the law became believers (like Paul and the other believing Pharisees), but some did not (like the Jewish religious leaders who later persecuted the believers); the same can be said about those who were not as zealous for the law (both the ordinary Jews who became believers and those who refused to believe). Similarly, their places of residence and the languages they spoke did not determine whether they became disciples of Jesus; there were Damascene and Judean Jews who became believers and those who rejected the gospel, and there were both Hebrew- and Greek- speaking Jews from different regions who became believers and those who refused to believe. The closest there was to a correlation was the people's commitment to Christ and their attitude toward Paul, but even this correlation is not really clear.

For ordinary Jewish believers, their primary concern was their safety. As long as they perceived Paul as an enemy and a persecutor of the believers, they could not be at-home with Paul, and Paul remained unhomed among them. When they began to see Paul as another disciple of Jesus, they also began to understand that Paul was one of them in Christ. For the religious authorities and Jews whose religious and political influences were jeopardized as the movement of Christ's followers began to grow, Paul's persecution of the believers was considered a positive move; when Paul himself became a disciple of Jesus, the apostle could no longer find a home among the members of the community where he previously belonged.

4

Unhomed Missionary to Galatia

In the previous chapter, we witnessed how Paul transformed from a zealous diasporan Jew who was thoroughly devoted to Judaism and the law to a zealous diasporan Jewish believer who was thoroughly devoted to Christ and the proclamation of the gospel. Paul's new commitment to Christ did not change his identity as a diasporan Jew nor did it lessen his commitment to God and to his Jewish roots. His new commitment to Christ transformed his understanding of God's work in history, his view about the purpose of the law, and, most especially, the expression of his zeal so that violence and religious extremism were no longer options as he propagated his theological views.

At-Home with the Hellenist Christians in Antioch

The death of Stephen and the persecution that ensued led to the proclamation of the gospel, not only in Judea and Samaria (Acts 8:1) but also to the Jews in Phoenicia (a coastal region east of the Mediterranean), Cyprus (an island west of Phoenicia), and Antioch of Syria (11:19).[1] The Gospel writers mention one family from Cyrene (part of modern-day Libya) who met Jesus: Simon of Cyrene, who helped Jesus carry his cross (Matt 27:32; Luke 23:26), together with his two sons, Alexander and Rufus (Mark 15:21). It is probable that they became believers after witnessing the death and resurrection of Jesus and eventually became pioneer evangelists in the North African city of Cyrene.[2] Luke

---

1. The presence of Jews in the region of Phoenicia is well attested (see Schnabel, *Acts*, 520). Likewise in Cyrene (see Barclay, *Jews in Mediterranean Diaspora*, 232–42) and Antioch (see Bruce, *The Book of Acts*, 224).

2. Richard Bauckham, *Jesus and the Eyewitnesses: The Gospels as Eyewitness Testimony* (Grand Rapids: Eerdmans, 2006), 51–52.

wrote that diasporan Jews from Cyprus and Cyrene also went to Antioch to proclaim the gospel to the Hellenists.[3]

The description, Hellenists, suggests two possible scenarios. The first scenario is that the first group of evangelists preached "only to Jews," that is, only to the Hebrew-speaking Jews, and the diasporan Jews from Cyrus and Cyrene spoke only to the Greek-speaking Jews. This first scenario makes sense if we consider the use of the term, Hellenist, in Acts 6:1 which distinguishes between Hebrew-speaking and Greek-speaking Jews in Jerusalem. One has to note that the contrast in Acts 6:1 is explicitly between the Hellenists (in Greek, *hellēnistēs*) and the Hebrews (in Greek, *hebraios*). However, in Acts 11:19–20, the contrast is between the Jewish evangelists from Jerusalem who preached "to no one except the Jews," and the diasporan Jewish evangelists from Cyprus and Cyrene who spoke to the Hellenists. This contrast leads to the second and more likely scenario, that the target audience of the Jewish evangelists from Jerusalem included the Greek-speaking Jews and those who preserved the use of their mother tongue, but not the Gentiles. This suggests that there might still have been some Jews who spoke Hebrew living in Antioch. Then the diasporan Jewish evangelists from Cyprus and Cyrene went to Antioch to preach the gospel, not only to the Jews but also to the Greek-speaking Gentiles. These Gentiles might have included both the proselytes who joined themselves to the Jewish synagogues,[4] and even the local Gentile residents of Antioch. This explains the origin of the first bilingual and multi-ethnic (Jews and Gentile) Christian church at Antioch.[5] In this way, the church of Antioch became an innovator in mission.[6]

The description of the church at Antioch in the previous paragraph is loaded with adjectives for the purpose of clarifying their ethnic composition and languages;[7] despite these descriptions, one must not lose sight that Luke focused only on one aspect of their identity, "And in Antioch the disciples

---

3. While the Jews in diaspora retain certain distinct characteristics, they have also considered themselves as "natives" of their host country. See Gruen, *Diaspora*, 242.

4. Josephus mentioned the growing number of Gentile proselytes to Judaism in the first century (*Jewish Wars* 7.3.3 §45).

5. The first group of leaders at Antioch was diverse. For sure, this is not comparable to modern society's attempt to be diverse and politically sensitive (Keener, *Acts*, 2:1985). Instead, it reflected a genuine and *organic* diversity resulting from their conviction that the gospel was to be proclaimed to all nations, languages, and tribes.

6. Ramsay, *Paul the Traveller*, 41.

7. Greek-speaking Christians from Jerusalem would naturally go to places where the use of Greek language and cultural diversity would be welcome. In addition, given the size of the Jewish community at Antioch, the evangelist also had a large audience (Keener, *Acts*, 2:1833, 1837).

were first called Christians" (11:26).⁸ The church at Antioch and the one in Jerusalem were both bilingual, and the accounts in Acts suggest that there were a significant number of Greek speakers in both cities. The primary difference between the Hellenists in Jerusalem that wanted to kill Paul (9:26–31) and the Hellenists in Antioch that welcomed him (11:25–26) was their belief in the Christ about whom Paul preached.

The apostles in Jerusalem welcomed this incident as a positive development so they sent Barnabas to be the pastor of the church at Antioch (11:22–24). Barnabas then sought Paul in Tarsus to be his coworker in this new and flourishing community of believers. Barnabas's recruitment of Paul is not surprising, considering that it was Barnabas who stood up for Paul when the latter was unwelcomed by the disciples in Jerusalem (9:26–27). Aside from the churches in Jerusalem, there must have been other local groups within the region of Judea. While the local congregation to which the apostles belonged welcomed Paul, there seems to have been other local congregations that did not, and Barnabas had to mediate between these disciples and Paul.⁹ The apostles in Jerusalem later acknowledged the ministry of Paul when he visited Jerusalem, as he revealed in one of his letters. He narrated, "when James and Cephas and John, who seemed to be pillars, perceived the grace that was given to me, they gave the right hand of fellowship to Barnabas and me, that we should go to the Gentiles and they to the circumcised" (Gal 2:9).

As a former zealous persecutor of the believers, Paul did not have a perfect track record but Barnabas knew of Paul's early ministry among the Jews in Damascus (Acts 9:22) and among the Hellenists in Jerusalem (9:27–29). As a bilingual diasporan Jew who could communicate in both Hebrew (21:40; 22:2) and Greek (as seen in his letters to the churches), Paul seemed to be a perfect fit for the ministry opening in Antioch: the earliest believing community was composed of diasporan Jews (many of them were Greek-speaking while some likely maintained their native Hebrew language), Greek-speaking proselytes, and Gentiles.¹⁰

---

8. It is difficult to tell how quickly the followers of the Way in other regions embraced this name. Even in the latter chapters of Acts, the Christian movement is still called "the Way" (Acts 19:23; 22:4; 24:14, 22). But we will refer to them as Christians henceforth.

9. Witherington, *Acts*, 325–26.

10. The church in Antioch of Syria became the first congregation of the diasporan Jews to send cross-cultural missionaries after Jesus commissioned his disciples to make disciples of all "Gentiles" (Greek, *ethnē*; Matt 28:18). The attitude of Antiochene Christians toward Gentiles should not be surprising. Aside from having a diverse group of leaders, as Keener explains, "Because synagogues in Antioch welcomed proselytes and God-fearers, it is not surprising that the Jewish Jesus movement in Antioch would do the same" (*Acts*, 2:1839). Being uncircumcised

For modern diasporan communities, their language and culture are what connect them to their origin. As Gema Ortega points out, language "de-territorializes 'home.'"[11] The same can be assumed for ancient Jewish diasporan communities. Language was what Paul shared in common with this mixed community in Antioch. This was the community that provided Paul a new home. This was Paul's "home church," to use modern parlance, which functioned as the "sending institution" that appointed Barnabas and Paul as their first missionaries (13:1–3). This was the community to which Barnabas and Paul were accountable, to whom they would give their "missionary report" after their stint in Galatia (14:24–27), and with whom they stayed when not on a mission (14:28).

At-Home with the Proconsul of Paphos

From the inland city of Antioch (Syria), the three missionaries led by the Holy Spirit (Barnabas, Paul and John [Mark]) left their home church and travelled to the port city of Seleucus to sail to Cyprus (Acts 13:4–5). Part of the reason that the Antiochenes heard the gospel was that Cypriot believers had gone there to preach the gospel (11:20). The Antiochene Christians returned the favor by sending evangelists to preach the gospel among the Cypriots, initially to the Jews living in the port city of Salamis (13:5). Barnabas himself was a diasporan Jew from Cyprus (4:36), so passing by the island for him meant preaching the gospel in his hometown to his friends, family, kinsmen, neighbors, and people close to him. Nothing is said about whether the Jews of Salamis accepted Paul's message, except that the gospel was proclaimed to them. From the eastern port city of Salamis, the three missionaries presumably travelled by land through the island of Cyprus to its western port city of Paphos, which might have required seven days' travel by foot.[12]

For the first time in Acts, the name "Paul" was used instead of his name "Saul" (13:9). This was probably the point when Paul began to take on more leadership roles than Barnabas. Henceforth, Luke referred to the missionary team as "Paul and his companions" (13:13). Interestingly, the story of Paul's mission to Salamis includes characters whose names bring to mind

---

might have placed the Gentiles at the lower tier in the unspoken (at least not yet at this point) hierarchy of membership. This issue would later be addressed as one of the first points of inquiries for the leaders in Jerusalem.

11. Gema Ortega, "Where is Home? Diaspora and Hybridity in Contemporary Dialogue," *Moderna Språk* 114, no. 4 (2020): 43.

12. Schnabel, *Acts*, 557.

protagonists in Luke–Acts, namely, the false prophet/magician, Elymas (a.k.a. Bar-Jesus), and the proconsul, Sergius Paulus (13:6–8). Ironically, the one nicknamed Bar-Jesus (or "son of Jesus" in Aramaic) was hindering the proconsul (whose Roman *cognomen*, the ancient equivalent to the modern surname, was Paul) from believing.[13] English translations typically retain the Latin form of the name Sergius Paulus to distinguish between the proconsul and the apostle, but Greek texts of Acts 13 do not make the differentiation. Both the proconsul and the apostle are called *Paulus*. This is why Luke explains that Saul "was *also* called Paul" (13:9, italics mine).

Luke noted that the name "Elymas" can be translated "magician." It is unclear from what language it was translated.[14] What is clear is that Elymas bar-Jesus had accommodated occultic practices while maintaining some devotion to Judaism. The real contrast in the story is between Elymas bar-Jesus, who was identified as "son of the devil . . . enemy of all righteousness . . . [one who is] full of all deceit and villainy" (13:10), and Paul, who was "filled with the Holy Spirit" (13:9). In short, the one who is called bar-Jesus (son of Jesus) was in actuality a son of the devil. Paul's identification of Elymas as a "son of the devil" shows that they came from different homes.

The failed attempt by Elymas to dissuade Sergius Paulus presents an image of two households trying to call people to be part of their families. It is no wonder that, on several occasions in his letter, Paul used the metaphor of adoption to describe the salvation experience of believers as they become incorporated into the family of faith (e.g. Rom 8:15–17, 23; Gal 4:4–7). The encounter between Paul and Elymas resulted in the proconsul believing (Acts 13:12). The apostle Paul then became at-home with the proconsul Paul but, most importantly, the proconsul Paul became at-home with the Lord, now an adopted member of the household of God.

At-Home with the Believing Jews and Proselytes, Unhomed with Unbelieving Jews in Pisidian Antioch. A Home for the Gentiles

From the island of Cyprus, Paul and Barnabas journeyed through the region north of the Mediterranean to the region of Galatia, establishing local churches

---

13. For a more detailed discussion on the identity of Sergius Paulus, see Foakes-Jackson and Lake, *Beginnings of Christianity*, 5:455–59.

14. For various suggestions, see BDAG, s.v., *Elumas*. It is also possible that the name derived from an ancient local Cyprian dialect that is unknown to us today.

in various cities we now call "the churches of Galatia,"[15] to whom Paul wrote his earliest letter in the NT. Upon reaching Perga in Pamphylia, their young companion John Mark decided to return to Jerusalem, leaving only Paul and Barnabas for the rest of the trip (13:13). Luke left the readers to speculate on the reason for John Mark's decision to leave,[16] but there were serious repercussions to this decision, which we will discuss later in this chapter. With only Paul and Barnabas left in the team, their first stop was the city of Antioch in Pisidia, where they had a mixed reception from the diasporan Jews (13:13–52).

Since both Paul and Barnabas were diasporan Jews from Tarsus and Cyprus, respectively, and the church that sent them was also composed predominantly of diasporan Jews from Antioch, it seems natural for them to want to start their work among the diasporan Jews wherever they went. So, even in Antioch of Pisidia, their initial work was among those in the Pisidian synagogue (13:14). The Pisidian Jews welcomed the missionaries, making them at-home.[17] Luke did not narrate any conversation the missionaries had with the leaders of the synagogue. We do know that Paul, despite being a visitor and a newcomer in the synagogue, was asked to share a "word of encouragement" with the congregation (13:15). Like Stephen, Paul briefly reviewed Israel's history (13:16–22), about which no one in the congregation would disagree, but the "word of encouragement" did not end with Paul reminding them of how God worked among their forefathers. Paul segued to John's baptism and his message of repentance, to Jesus's death and resurrection, and to Christ's offer of forgiveness and the limitations of the law of Moses (13:23–41). The last part of the message could have potentially angered devout Jews, but the initial response of many Jews and proselytes was positive for they asked the two missionaries to come back the following Sabbath so they could hear more. Paul and Barnabas encouraged them in Jesus as they left (13:42–43).

When Paul and Barnabas returned the next Sabbath, the turnout seemed to be higher than expected, because the people in attendance included "crowds" (13:45) and, as Luke described it, "the whole city gathered to hear the word

---

15. Bruce explains that Pisidian Antioch was so called because it was near Pisidia, but actually lay in Phrygia, which belonged to the kingdom of Galatia. See his *Book of Acts*, 251; see especially 251–52, nn. 35–36).

16. Some have speculated that Mark was unhappy that Paul was beginning to take over the missionary work, "replacing" Barnabas. See Schnabel, *Acts*, 573.

17. It is well attested that Roman officials treated the members of Jewish synagogues with high regard (Keener, *Acts*, 2:1463). The good reputation of the diasporan Jews could invite even Gentiles to be patrons for their synagogues. See Tessa Rajak, "Synagogue Within the Greco-Roman City," in *Jews, Christians, and Polytheists in Ancient Synagogue: Cultural Interaction in the Greco-Roman Period*, ed. Stephen Fine (London: Routledge, 1999), 161–63.

of the Lord" (13:44). This may suggest that the believing Jews and proselytes invited friends with them to the meeting. Ironically, the Jews were not angered by Paul's comment about the limitations of the law but the immediate impact his message had on the Pisidians. It was jealousy that motivated them to contradict Paul's message (13:45). Paul's zeal (Greek, *zēlos*) led him to persecute the church (22:3–5). Similarly, the "jealousy" (Greek, *zēlos*; the same Greek word for "zeal") of the Jews led them to rally the influential people of Pisidian Antioch to persecute Paul and drive them out of the city (13:50). Keener expounds on this "jealousy" this way

> What appealed to the Gentiles, however, could prove offensive to the synagogue's base constituents. Further, many of the Gentile adherents, though unable to be full members of the synagogue, were benefactors whose transfer of support (if the synagogue community itself rejected the apostolic message) would stir opposition (cf. Acts 13:45, 50; 17:12). Gentiles who had already taken the step of full conversion (for males, including circumcision) may also not have been pleased by a newer, "lower" standard for other Gentiles. Possibly the higher-status members of the synagogues (13:15) or these high-status God-fearers were able to stir others with status against the outsiders (13:50).[18]

A week earlier, these diasporan Jewish missionaries seemed to have found a new temporary home. It did not take long for Paul and Barnabas to influence the members of the Pisidian synagogue and even the residents of the city. As a result, the Jews led the more influential residents to persecute the missionaries, and thus they became unhomed. Clearly, the cause of rejection was not the teachings of Paul but the loss of influence of some Pisidian Jews. Their rejection made it clear to Paul that their work would include, for a large part, the Gentiles (13:36) and that their ministry would be "to the ends of the earth" (13:47; cf. 1:8). Although the unbelieving Pisidian Jews who were hanging on to their influence made Paul and Barnabas unhomed, the duo were able to influence the local Pisidians to find home with the Lord, and they continue to spread the message throughout their home region (13:46–49).

---

18. Keener, *Acts*, 2:2095.

At-Home with the Believers, Unhomed Among Unbelieving Jews and Gentiles at Iconium

After Paul and Barnabas were unhomed in Pisidian Antioch, they "shook the dust from their feet against [those who persecuted them]" (13:51; cf. Matt 10:14; Mark 6:11; Luke 9:5; 10:11) and moved to the next city, Iconium. Once again, Paul and Barnabas joined the local synagogue as was their practice (Acts 14:1). That Paul and Barnabas began with the Jewish synagogue clarified that their earlier statement, "we are turning to the Gentiles" (13:46), did not mean that they planned to abandon their outreach to the diasporan Jews, but that their work would be more inclusive of the Gentiles, whether they were proselytes or not. As evidenced in their work at Iconium, the distinction was no longer between the Hebrews (Hebrew-speaking Jews) and Hellenists (Greek-speaking Jews) in Jerusalem (6:1). The comparison is closer to the distinction between the Jews (which might have included both Hebrew- and Greek-speaking Jews) and the Hellenists (Greek-speaking foreigners living among the Jews) at Antioch of Syria (11:19–20). At Iconium, there were diasporan Jews (some of whom might have retained their native Hebrew language while others were Greek-speakers) and Greeks (*hellēn*, not *hellēnistēs* or "Greek-speakers") which might have included native residents or foreigners dwelling with them (14:1). The latter belonged to what the ancient Jews referred to as *ethnos* ("nations" or "Gentiles").

When Paul and Barnabas began their work in the synagogue at Iconium,[19] the Greeks who believed their message together with the Jews were presumably proselytes (14:1). It seems that some Jews were not persuaded (Greek, *apeitheō*) by their message,[20] and these were the ones who "poisoned the mind" (Greek, *ekakōsan tas psuchas*, literally, "did evil to the soul") of those who believed (14:2).[21] Unlike the unbelieving group in Pisidia, those in Iconium seemed unable to persuade many to reject the message of Paul and Barna-

---

19. The expression "synagogue" can refer either to the structure where the believers meet or to the congregation (Gruen, *Diaspora*, 108). This is comparable to the use of the term "church." While one may continue to argue that the Greek *ekklēsia* refers only to the people, the church is commonly used to refer to both the building and the people.

20. The same word can be translated as "disobey" (BDAG, s.v. *apeitheō*). This suggests that obedience results from one being convinced to do the right thing, because the one who is unpersuaded will be disobedient.

21. The English parlance carries a connotation of cultural solidarity among members of one ethnic group that causes individual members to think similarly. As Joseph Mitsuo Kitagawa puts it, "every individual, and every culture and people, lives not only in the geographical, psychic world but also in what might be termed world of meaning." See his "The Asian Mind," *Anglican and Episcopal History* 65, no. 4 (1996): 404. Any idea that challenges the culturally accepted belief can be dangerous. From an ancient Greek perspective, it is also harmful for the soul.

bas. As a result, Paul and Barnabas were able to stay there longer, preaching and performing miracles among the residents of Iconium (14:3),[22] both Jews and Gentiles.

Eventually, the residents were convinced by the unbelieving group; even their officials began to be convinced, and so Paul and Barnabas were no longer welcome to stay. The local residents, the diasporan Jews, and even the officials got involved in the process (14:5). The attempt to stone them need not be interpreted as an act comparable to what Stephen experienced. Stephen was considered a blasphemer worthy of death. Paul and Barnabas, however, were not branded as blasphemers. Thus, the attempt to stone them can be considered as more a way to harass them into thinking twice regarding whether they would continue their activities in the city.[23] Once again, they were unhomed and had to move to the Lycaonian cities of Lystra and Derbe (14:5–7).

Unhomed with the Non-Believers at Lystra, At-Home with the Disciples at Derbe

The miracles that Paul and Barnabas performed at Iconium were only mentioned in passing by Luke (Acts 14:3). In contrast, he placed more significance on the miracle witnessed by the Lycaonians – because it was the deciding factor in the Lycaonians' response to them (14:8–12). The healing of the lame man caused the Lycaonians to welcome the two missionaries and to mistake them for gods (14:12). Luke noted that the local residents spoke in Lycanonian

---

22. Paul's mission to Iconium was the basis for the apocryphal Acts of Paul and Thecla. The canonical version does not include personal names, while the apocryphal version is more elaborate. In the latter, Thecla, a young girl betrothed to Thamyris, heard Paul preach and believed his message. She decided to call off the wedding so she could follow Paul. Her mother, Theoclia, expressed her frustration to Thamyris because they were losing influence over Thecla and the youth of the city, saying, "Thamyris, this man will overturn the city of the Iconians and your Thecla too; for all the women and the young men go in to him to be taught by him." See Acts of Paul and Thecla 9. As a result, Thecla's family had Paul imprisoned, where he continued preaching. While in prison, the young girl would visit the apostle to listen to him preach. Paul was eventually released, and Thecla continued as one of the first female evangelists who ministered in Iconium. There are numerous details in the two accounts that are different, like the account of Paul's imprisonment and the motivation of the unbelievers in persecuting Paul. However, some details can be complementary, like the length of their stay in the city, which allows Thecla a significant amount of time to follow Paul around. If the story of Thecla is true, it would explain how there was a continuous Christian witness even after Paul and Barnabas left the city.

23. Schnabel, *Acts*, 605.

(14:11),[24] which suggests that the two missionaries did not understand what was said. Language barriers are often obvious reasons for miscommunication and misunderstanding: additional factors further prevent one from welcoming "the other." In this case, however, while Paul and Barnabas did not understand what the Lycaonians said, they clearly understood the gist of what they were shouting, and their actions were comprehensible. This incident shows that while language can be a barrier to communication, it need not be a barrier to hospitality. Even the priest from the temple of Zeus welcomed them (14:13). This action could be interpreted as a form of invitation for them to reside with the people, for where else should deities dwell but in the temples dedicated to them. In other words, for the priest of Zeus to welcome them is a way of offering them a "home" among the locals. The Lycaonians' hospitality toward the missionaries they mistook as gods is not surprising. There is an old tale by Ovid about a pious couple, Philemon and Baucis, who entertained Jupiter and Mercury (the Roman equivalent of the Greek gods, Zeus and Hermes) and they were rewarded for their hospitality.[25] Moreover, this kind of hospitality is also found in Scripture (for example, Abraham in Genesis 18; the author of Hebrews also exhorts believers to hospitality [Heb 13:2]).

Unlike in other cities that Paul and Barnabas visited, their primary audience in Lystra of Lycaonia were Gentiles who worshipped the Greek gods, Zeus and Hermes (Acts 14:12).[26] In Paul's message to them, he did not appeal to Israel's history, but to the story of creation (14:15), a history that the Jews and Gentiles shared in common. Finding common grounds was Paul's expression of hospitality toward the people he was reaching for the gospel; this is evidenced in his references to shared identity, ancestry, and history with the diasporan Jews of Pisidia (13:14–41), a shared humanity and human origins with the Gentiles of Lycaonia (14:15–17), and also later with the Gentiles of Athens (17:22–32). The residents of Lystra were insistent on offering sacrifices to the two missionaries (14:18), a kind of hospitality that they could not accept.

---

24. Strabo identifies four indigenous languages used in the region near the border areas of Asia and Lycia in addition to Greek: Pisidian, Solymian, Carian, and Lydian (Strabo, *Geography* 13.1.65; 14.2.3–8). This suggests that even in other places, the native dialects were still preserved, as in the case of Lycaonian. See Schnabel, *Acts*, 607.

25. Bruce, *The Book of Acts*, 274.

26. Deissmann observes that Jewish synagogues scattered throughout the Mediterranean functioned as a silent protest against the polytheistic local cultures, see his *Paul*, 86. The presence of pagan temples inevitably posited a challenge to their monotheistic message. It seems that when Paul arrived at Lystra the devotees of Zeus were more influential than the Jews.

The unbelieving Jews from Pisidian Antioch and Iconium were not satisfied on driving Paul and Barnabas out of their city. They clearly wanted the missionaries dead, but they were unsuccessful in executing their plans (13:50–51; 14:5–7). What is noteworthy is that the unbelieving Jews from Pisidian Antioch and Iconium would travel as far as Lystra, a distance of about 100 miles (160 kilometers) to pursue Paul and Barnabas.[27] When the pursuers reached Lystra, they convinced the crowd to stone Paul (14:19), however, while they succeeded in stoning him, they failed to kill him (14:19). So, the two missionaries were able to visit the other Lycaonian city of Derbe where they were welcomed by those who believed (14:21–23). The distance between these two cities is more than sixty miles (about 100 kilometers).[28] The brief description of Paul's travel from Lystra to Derbe should not cover up the long and arduous journey the apostle took to run away from an angry mob, instead of getting medical attention. In other words, in order to save his life, Paul either had to run away from the crowd who wanted to kill him and risk aggravating his health after being stoned and left half-dead or get medical attention within the city and risk being caught by the mob who were seeking his life. This was the extent of his being unhomed in Lystra – an experience he did not have to endure in Derbe. No wonder that just before Paul appointed elders at Lystra and left them, he encouraged the believers by "saying that through many tribulations we must enter the kingdom of God" (14:22).

Luke did not specify how long they stayed at Derbe, but it was long enough for Paul to recover, for the two to again make disciples, and to allow the situation to cool down so that they could return to the cities they previously visited to appoint elders there (14:21–23). In other words, Paul and Barnabas were unhomed at Iconium and Lystra, but they found a period of solace in Derbe.

Back to Their Home Church

When their first mission circuit was over it was time for the missionaries to go back to their home church to give a ministry update. Because the church at Antioch was home to Paul and Barnabas, it is not surprising that "they remained no little time with the disciples" (14:28). Paul's return trip from Derbe to Syria required them to travel through the main Roman road passing through "Dalisandos, Kodylessos, Posala, Ilistra, and Laranda, cities in

---

27. Barrett, *The Acts of the Apostles*, 1:683.
28. Barrett, *The Acts of the Apostles*, 1:685.

which they may also have preached the gospel."[29] It is possible that they chose to travel by land in order to visit his home region.[30] The main focus of their report was twofold: what God did through them, "and how he had opened a door of faith to the Gentiles" (14:27). This was a significant development for from that point onwards the gospel would no longer be exclusive to the Jews in Jerusalem, the diasporan Jews, and the Gentile proselytes who decided to adopt the Jewish way of life. The door of faith was opened for the Gentiles to enter. These were people who had little to no prior exposure to the Jewish faith or to the Christian message.

The idiom Luke used is telling. The opening of doors implies hospitality, like a host welcoming a visitor into their home. The ministry of Paul and Barnabas did one important thing: it opened a way for the Gentiles to find a home in the Lord through faith. God is the active agent who opened the "door of faith." The indirect object in the Greek sentence, *tois ethnesin*, can be classified under what grammarians call the "dative of advantage" so that the expression can be rendered "for the benefit of the nations/Gentiles." Since God opened the door of faith for the benefit of the Gentiles, through the proclamation of the gospel the Gentiles can find a home with the Lord. The inclusion of the Gentiles who were non-proselytes posed an issue for Jewish believers who considered their faith in Christ as fully embedded in Judaism; this led to the conflict between the two missionaries and the Judaizers, and the first ever council to settle a theological dispute.

Home Redefined in Christ, Hospitality for Gentiles in Galatia

While Paul and Barnabas were still in their home church at Antioch, men from Jerusalem who were devoted to Judaism disputed with them. The point of their discussion was not whether Jesus died and resurrected, nor was it about Jesus's identity as Christ and the savior. Presumably, these men accepted these as truths that they could believe (see Acts 15:5). The issue was also not whether Jewish Christians should abandon Judaism; at this point, the Jews did not have a problem remaining in Judaism while professing their faith in Jesus. The point of discussion was the place of the Mosaic law in the process, especially after the "door of faith" was opened for the uncircumcised Gentiles and they were joining the community of believers. Unfortunately, the men from Judea were

---

29. Schnabel, *Acts*, 613.

30. Jerome Murphy-O'Connor, "On the Road and on the Sea with St. Paul," *Bible Review* 1, no. 2 (1985): 46.

trying to make the "door of faith" that God had opened for the non-proselyte Gentiles *unnecessarily* narrow. This is not the kind of narrow gate (Matt 7:13-14) or narrow door (Luke 13:24) to which Jesus referred. Circumcision was the physical mark required by God for Israel as an external sign that one was a member of the "people of God,"[31] and this was the same requirement the Jewish traditionalists were trying to impose on the Gentiles. In other words, the men of Judea tried to shut out and displace people that God had welcomed to be at-home with him.

Aside from the Jews regularly attending the synagogues at Antioch of Syria, God-fearers were also incorporated into the body of believers. These God-fearers belonged to the community of Gentiles, who were what Bruce Chilton calls "idol-worshipping, sometimes pig-eating subjects of Rome who had views of Judaism that ranged from incomprehension to outright prejudice."[32] Whether the Christian community should welcome the Gentiles was already settled with Peter's vision of the unclean animals (10:9–48). The more important question now was what to do with those who were willing to be baptized? Chilton responds to this question.

> Antioch pressed the logic of Peter's vision to its limit – and beyond. The simple fact is, he did not authorize baptizing pagans. Questions and problems emerged immediately from what happened in Antioch. If Gentiles were to be immersed in Jesus's name, how much did they have to know about him, and what aspects of Israelite religion were they to acknowledge and practice? Teachers such as Barnabas shared Peter's vision and accepted its authority, but they had no policy to deal with the situation in Antioch.[33]

Paul received a similar message from God concerning the inclusion of the Gentiles as members of God's people. He narrated his spiritual journey in the autobiographical section of his letter to the Galatians. He claimed to have received the message he preached through divine revelation (Gal 1:12). This message challenged his misplaced religious zeal (1:13–14), but definitely did not challenge him to total abandonment of his Jewish traditions. The fact that Paul did not leave Judaism made this clear. Nonetheless, Paul narrated that this revelation had to do with the preaching of the gospel to the Gentiles,

---

31. James D. G. Dunn, *The New Perspective on Paul*, rev. ed. (Grand Rapids: Eerdmans, 2005), 155.
32. Bruce Chilton, *Rabbi Paul: An Intellectual Biography* (New York: Doubleday, 2004), 103.
33. Chilton, *Rabbi Paul*, 103–4.

and, by implication, their inclusion within the people of God. So, Paul shared, "[God] was pleased to reveal his Son to me, in order that I might preach him among the Gentiles" (1:16).

Paul did not explicate the contents of this revelation, but it must have raised sufficient questions about his previously held views that he thought it was necessary to take some time alone, presumably to reflect upon these matters, and then consult the apostles in Jerusalem about them (1:17–19). He later visited Jerusalem together with Barnabas and Titus (2:1–2) and as Paul recounted the visit he only highlighted one thing: Titus, the Gentile, was not forced to be circumcised (2:3). This suggests that the divine revelation, Paul's personal reflection, and his consultation with the other apostles led him to conclude that the circumcision of Gentiles should not be a requirement for them to belong to Christ. This was one of the aspects of "freedom in Christ" that Paul disseminated – that the uncircumcised Gentiles did not need to be circumcised to belong to Christ. Hence, Paul and Peter agreed about the basic scope of their apostolic ministry: Paul to the uncircumcised and Peter to the circumcised (2:7–9).

In his letter to the Galatian churches, Paul clarified several important truths: that *in Christ*, God's promises to Abraham were made available to the Gentiles (3:14); that *in Christ*, there is neither Jew nor Greek, both groups can be considered children of God (3:26–28); and that *in Christ*, circumcision and uncircumcision make no difference (5:6). N. T. Wright explains, "Paul takes it for granted that the Messiah, the ultimate representative Jew, has created in himself a new people, a new home, a new temple, a new way of life in which all the moral distinctives between Jew and pagan would be maintained."[34] God did not only find himself a home among the Gentiles, but allowed the Gentiles to be at-home in him.

The Galatians were lured to abandon Paul's message about their freedom in Christ in favor of the message of circumcision (5:1–15). By accepting the message that circumcision is necessary to be part of God's people, the Galatians had actually deserted (Greek, *metatithēmi*) Christ (1:6). Ironically, in their desire to be at-home with Christ by following the circumcision group, the Galatians had "displaced" themselves from the place they wanted to belong. In other words, the message of the circumcision group, while attempting to incorporate the Gentiles into the "people of God," has actually caused them to be displaced or unhomed from Christ. The gravity of the offence was great, so

---

34. N. T. Wright, *Paul and the Faithfulness of God*, Christian Origins and the Question of God 4 (Minneapolis: Fortress Press, 2013), 1088.

no wonder Paul declared that if anyone preaches a message that causes such displacement, "let him be accursed" (1:8–9). To be accursed (Greek, *anathema*) also implies being separated or displaced from Christ.[35] Paul's message to the Galatians was not so much about Christ finding a home in the believers' hearts, but more about the believers finding a home *in Christ*. In the process, Paul redefined what it means to be at-home and to belong to the people of God, and that is to be *in Christ*.

The revelation Paul received confirmed the revelation Peter received, but it still did not answer the question concerning Gentiles who were baptized in the name of Jesus. This was the question that had to be settled by the leadership in Jerusalem.

At-Home with the Believers in Phoenicia and Samaria, Unhomed Among Judaizers, At-Home with the Churches in Jerusalem. A Home for the Gentiles

The dispute between Paul and Barnabas with the Judaizers caused such dissension that the Antiochenes concluded that this was not a matter that they should settle on their own but must involve the apostles and elders in Jerusalem, so they sent Paul and Barnabas to represent them (Acts 15:2). On their way from Antioch of Syria to Jerusalem, the duo visited the believers in Phoenicia and Samaria.[36] These were the disciples who came to faith after the death of Stephen resulted in the scattering of the believing Jews who then proclaimed the gospel wherever they went (8:1; 11:19).

The early Christians might not have enjoyed the kind of technology for networking that we have today, but it seems they found a way to do so through visitations and letter writing. Paul's visit to Phoenicia and Samaria with Barnabas was the first record of their visit after Paul became a believer of Jesus. The reputation of Barnabas had been impeccable from the beginning, and Paul was no longer a dreaded persecutor but one who was at the forefront of Gentile mission. The two missionaries reported to the Christians in Phoenicia and Samaria the same report they presented to their home church in Syria. This report was well-received by the Phoenician and Samaritan Christians (15:3). It is important to keep in mind that the composition of the churches in Phoenicia and Samaria was different from that in Jerusalem. Given that Phoenicia was

---

35. BDAG, s.v. *anathēma*.
36. Gruen expounds on the various (and inconsistent) ancient accounts on how the Jews landed in Phoenicia (*Diaspora*, 236–37, esp. nn. 37–41).

not a Jewish territory, the earliest congregation was likely a mixed community with Jews, proselytes, and local Phoenicians (Gentiles). Similarly, the Samaritan congregation mght have had some Jews and proselytes, with a majority of Samaritans. These ethnic and cultural elements are undeniable reasons why the Phoenician, Samaritan, and even the Syrian Christians found it easier to welcome the Gentiles into the church.

This kind of hospitality did not seem to have come naturally to the congregation in Jerusalem. The believing Pharisees among them refused to welcome Gentiles unless they became like Jews by accommodating their practice of circumcision (15:5). At the heart of this issue was still *power and control wrapped in theological and doctrinal packaging*. Keener laments, "The insistence of these Pharisees highlights the problem of centralization (cf. 7:2–3, 9–10, 33): to what degree should the vote of the local church in Jerusalem, influenced by local concerns, shape the future of other local churches struggling with different, often conflicting concerns?"[37]

It took a heavenly vision to convince even Peter that God desired the Gentiles to be part of his people, and the issue of circumcision was not then even on the table. There were disciples in Jerusalem who considered the spiritual significance of circumcision as more important than the outward rite, and hence, were more welcoming toward uncircumcised Gentiles, but they seemed to "have formed a negligible minority."[38] Moreover, while the apostles, elders, and the rest of the congregation welcomed Paul and Barnabas, the idea that the whole Christian movement should include the uncircumcised and "unclean" Gentiles was not accepted without struggle, as Peter himself narrated (15:7–12).

In Acts, the inclusion of Gentiles among God's people is clear even from the beginning.

1. Jesus's post-resurrection commission to the apostles specified the Gentiles as recipients of the gospel message, "But you will receive power when the Holy Spirit has come upon you, and you will be my witnesses in Jerusalem and in all Judea and Samaria, and to the end of the earth" (1:8).

2. With the diasporan Jews "from under every nation under heaven" (2:5) being recipients of the gospel message, they presumably went

---

37. Keener, *Acts*, 3:2229.

38. Bruce, *The Book of Acts*, 287. It is also possible that the Gentiles within the community were regarded by the Jewish traditionalists as having similar standing as the God-fearers within the community. See James D. G. Dunn, *Beginning From Jerusalem*, Christianity in the Making 2 (Grand Rapids: Eerdmans, 2009), 445.

back to their host nations after the celebration of the Pentecost to spread the same message. Peter himself testified, "For the promise is for you and for your children and *for all who are far off, everyone whom the Lord our God calls to himself*" (2:39, italics mine). The phrase "for all who are far off" and the word "everyone" included not only the Jews in diaspora but also anyone from their host country who would receive the message of God's salvation.

3. The conflict between the Hebrew- and Greek-speaking Jews in Acts 6:1 should not be considered a small matter. While the early church can be commended on how they settled the conflict,[39] the fact that the conflict was between two groups with the same ethnicity but different languages is a clear sign of their struggle to mingle with "the other," yet at the same time, an early testament that, in the end, God's people will be composed of people from every tribe and language (Rev 5:9; 13:7; 14:6).

4. The delay of the Spirit's descent upon the Samaritans also showed that the people of God would not be composed only of Jews and proselytes but also those outside these categories. After Philip preached the gospel to the Samaritans, they were baptized but did not receive the Spirit as the believers did in Acts 2. The Spirit came upon the believers only when Peter and John came to Samaria and laid their hands on them (8:14–17). The delay was a way for God to confirm to the leaders of the church in Jerusalem that the Spirit who descended upon the Jews in Jerusalem is the same one received by the Samaritans. As a result, even the apostles began to include the Samaritans in their proclamation (8:25). There was no such delay in Acts 10 when the Gentiles heard the message, perhaps because Peter was there to witness the outpouring (10:44–48).

5. The dispersed Jews had been preaching to Gentiles prior to the sending of Paul to the Gentiles: Philip preached to the Ethiopian eunuch (8:26–40) and Peter preached to Cornelius (10:1–43).

As readers of Acts, these stories are readily available for us to see, but it was not so for the Jewish Christians in Jerusalem, at least not until the inclusion

---

39. Todd Penner posits that the purpose of recounting the story of conflict in Acts 6 is to show how the early Christian community handled conflicts properly. See his *In Praise of Christian Origin: Stephen and the Hellenists in Lukan Apologetic History*, Emory Studies in Early Christianity (New York: T&T Clark, 2004), 262–76.

of Gentiles as God's people was openly discussed among them. Interestingly, the venue for discussing this important issue was the turf of those who advocated for circumcision. The council eventually favored the "visitors," not the "home team," so to speak. As mentioned earlier, while the Lord's work among the Gentiles was clear, even Peter admitted to having struggled to accept this development (15:7–12; cf. 10:9–33; 11:1–18). The pressure from those who insisted that Gentiles must be circumcised must have been so strong that, even years after the meeting, Peter once again succumbed to their pressure, as Paul narrated (Gal 2:11–14).

The Christian Jews in Jerusalem had to face this important reality. It is clear that the main issue was not whether Gentiles could be part of their group. Their real concern was whether the Gentiles could be accepted without being like them in their commitment to the law of Moses. After deliberating, the leaders of the Jerusalem church concluded that they should not burden the Gentiles by requiring them to keep the law, except for a few things pertaining to their moral and religious practices and dietary concerns that might have prevented table fellowship with the Jews.[40] This was a positive development because it enabled the Gentile Christians to be at-home with the church in Jerusalem.

Unhomed with Barnabas

After spending some time in their home church at Antioch, Paul invited Barnabas to visit the Galatian churches once again (Acts 15:36). Like they did the first time, Barnabas wanted to bring John Mark with them, but Paul refused (15:37–38). We can infer from their points of contention that their separation became inevitable because of the differences in their ministry priorities: for Barnabas, loyalty and forgiveness; for Paul, wholehearted commitment.[41] As a result, Barnabas went back to his homeland of Cyprus with John Mark (15:39) and Paul took Silas with him to Syria and Cilicia (15:40–41). So, the two went their separate ways.

Barrett suspects that John Mark's family was "of some importance in the church of Jerusalem," and that Mark's role was not just as an apprentice in-charge of the material needs of the team, but that he might have had some

---

40. Several Second Temple and Rabbinic writings contain provisions for Gentiles wishing to join the believing Jewish community, and there are common themes seen in these works: moral requirements, religious/worship practice, and dietary requirements. See chart in Keener, *Acts*, 3:2266.

41. Keener, *Acts*, 3:2299.

teaching role as well.[42] It is possible that Barnabas saw Mark's potential, while Paul saw the impediments that Mark could cause their mission. The result of their disagreement was to move in different directions.

Ethnic Barriers and Being Unhomed

As the story of Paul's work as a missionary continued to unfold in Luke's narrative, a pattern of problems also began to emerge. Ethnic barriers, and by extension, language barriers, are definitely a challenge for anyone, especially those, like Paul, doing cross-cultural ministry. Ethnic tensions existed between the Jews and the Samaritans. It was candidly discussed in the Gospels (John 4:9), and there is no reason to think that this was not an issue two decades later, when Paul was doing his ministry. Moreover, the insistence by some devout Jews that Gentiles be circumcised suggests that ethnic markers remained a crucial factor for some devout Jews as they decided who to welcome into their community and who to reject. The sons of Jacob were the first to require Gentiles to be circumcised, but they did not do it to genuinely welcome Shechem and his people. They were just looking for opportunities to avenge Dinah (Gen 34:1–31). Paul's contemporaries were willing to welcome Gentiles, but they operated on the same set of principles – be like us (34:15), we will not become like you! This is not about cultural practices and values that clearly go against the teachings of the Scripture, but the unwillingness on the part of the missionaries to be flexible, to listen and observe, and learn. It is also about the urge of the gospel heralds to make their listeners "in their own image" and to use Scripture as a pretext to do so. This is the reason why Paul's missionary principle of becoming all things to all people (1 Cor 9:22) was truly revolutionary.

Having said these things, while one cannot deny that racial, ethnic, and language tensions are real challenges for Christian missionaries, in Paul's case, these were not the bottom line issues. The fact that the diasporan Jews were able to adapt well with the natives of their region and the Gentiles were able to also associate with the Jews in Judea shows that the animosity between them was motivated by something more than just their racial differences and communication gaps. From the accounts that Luke included in his narrative, power and influence were reasons for the hostile treatment of others. For example, the attempt of Elymas to dissuade the proconsul from believing Paul illustrates a kind of spiritual battle, a power struggle between the Holy Spirit and the "son

---

42. Barrett, *The Acts of the Apostles*, 1:612.

of the devil" (Acts 13:9–10) in the form of a power to influence the proconsul. This authority to influence is also seen in the discussion between Paul and the Judaizers. If the Gentiles were no longer required to be circumcised, the influence of the Jews over the Gentile believers would also diminish. More to the point, the discussion in Acts 15 about whether the Gentiles must be circumcised was more than just a matter of interpreting the law, it also included the extent to which the Jewish majority had authority over the incoming Gentile minority within the church.

5

Unhomed Missionary to Greece and Asia Minor

In the previous chapters, we saw how Paul maintained his commitment to the God of his forefathers and how his zeal was transformed from one who was *willing to kill* to one who was *willing to die* for his beliefs. His missionary work among the Galatians also refined his theological stance on the place of the Gentiles in the plan of God.

Paul's ministry constantly placed him in an unhomely place or a state of ambivalence, wherein he experienced hospitality from some and hostility from others. Ethnic, racial, and language barriers were real factors that made him at-home or unhomed within a community. Religious affiliation was a more crucial consideration. One often overlooked factor in discussions about Paul's ministry and the suffering he endured is power and influence. This is the pattern that emerged as Paul continued his ministry as an apostle among the Jews in the diaspora and the Gentile natives of their host regions. This same factor continued to manifest in Paul's second missionary journey.

The Jewish Home of Timothy and Being At-Home with the Lycaonian Jews

After separating with Barnabas who took Mark with him to his hometown of Cyprus to continue missionary work there (Acts 15:39), Paul took Silas with him to revisit the churches he and Barnabas had started earlier (15:40–41). While in Lystra, they met the young Timothy whose father was a Greek and his mother was a Jew. Nothing else was said about Timothy's father except that he was a Greek,[1] presumably local Lystran, who married a diasporan Jew. There are hints, however, in the letters of Paul that while the family of Timothy lived among the Greeks, they continued to hold on to their Jewish faith (2 Tim 1:5).[2] This suggests that while Timothy grew up in a Lycaonian community who believed in gods like Zeus and Hermes, and in a city with a temple dedicated to these deities (Acts 14:11–13), he was raised in a Jewish home where he received religious training. His mother and grandmother, however, were understandably not able to fulfil all the requirements of the law, and so Timothy was not circumcised according to Jewish law.

We earlier noted that the issue of circumcision was the main point of contention between Paul and some devoted Jews who insisted that the rite was necessary for a person to be part of God's people. As discussed in the previous chapter, Paul advocated for the Gentile believers, saying that they should not be alienated for being uncircumcised. Paul recalled one incident relating to this issue, "But even Titus, who was with me, was not forced to be circumcised, though he was a Greek" (Gal 2:3). For Paul, a Gentile's circumcision was not necessary for belonging since God had extended his hospitality to both Jews and Gentiles alike. This raises the question as to why Paul had Timothy circumcised. If Paul did not require Silas to be circumcised because Silas was a Gentile, the only logical explanation as to why he required Timothy to be circumcised is that he did not consider his young associate as a Gentile but as a Jew, despite being from a multiracial background. As a Gentile, it was *not necessary* for Silas to be circumcised. As a son of a Jewish mother, even if his father was not a Jew, it was *not prohibited* for Timothy to be circumcised but, as a minister to the diasporan Jews, it seemed wise for Timothy to be circumcised, especially considering that the Jews knew his father was a Greek (16:3).

Luke did not provide details on the whereabouts of Timothy's Greek father at this time and how Paul was able to convince him to allow his son to be circumcised. This development is presumably something Timothy's mother and grandmother would have gladly welcomed as diasporan Jews living within a Greek household. Timothy's circumcision was done, as Luke narrated, "because of the Jews who were in those places, for they all knew that his father was a

---

1. Schnabel opines that Timothy's father might have been an uncircumcised God-fearer and member of the synagogue who prevented Timothy's circumcision (*Acts*, 665).

2. In addition, Tannaitic sources consider children of Jewish mothers as Jews (Mishnah, Qiddushin 3:12; Yebamot 7:5; Tosefta, Qiddushin 4:16), as many scholars have noted. See Keener, *Acts*, 3:2317, nn. 193–94.

Greek" (Acts 16:3). Paul's decision to circumcise Timothy allowed Timothy to be at-home with the Lycaonian Jews.

At-Home with Lydia, Unhomed with the Fortune-Telling Business Owners, At-Home with the Jailer at Philippi

Having revisited the believers in regions of Phrygia and Galatia, Paul was set to start his work with Silas and Timothy in the next region to the west, which was Asia. This step makes sense strategically. From Syria, going westward from one region to the next nearest would eventually take him to Rome (Rom 1:15; 15:22–24), which was his plan. As Paul put it, to preach the gospel to the Gentiles "from Jerusalem and all the way around to Illyricum" (15:19).³ However, instead of proceeding from Phrygia and Galatia to Asia, they went northwest to Mysia because they were "forbidden by the Holy Spirit to speak the word in Asia" (Acts 16:6). Their attempt to go to Bithynia (which is east of Mysia) seems to be an attempt to fulfil their earlier plan to do missions in Asia (which is south of Bithynia). Once again, the Spirit did not allow them (16:7). Luke did not elaborate how Paul and his team knew that it was the Spirit's prohibition. Rather, he implied through the vision of the "Macedonian man" (16:9) that the reason was that God planned for them work in Macedonia first. Thus, the team set out from Troas for Macedonia and began their work in Philippi.

Interestingly, the first "Macedonian man" Paul encountered turned out to be a group of Jewish Macedonian women. Paul was met with hospitality by some female devotees who frequented a "place of prayer" near the riverside. These women were there on a Sabbath (16:13), so there is a chance that this group was composed of diasporan Jews and proselytes who met for prayer.⁴ Jews required men to lead synagogues, which may explain why Luke specified that the group led by Lydia was not the synagogue, but a prayer group.⁵ In his

---

3. This expression reflects Paul's idea of the boundaries of the Roman world (Deissmann, *Paul*, 35). If this is the case, then the expression "Jerusalem to Illyricum" can be interpreted to mean "the Roman Empire," which is the target of Paul's missionary activity.

4. Gruen identifies both the *proseuche* (lit. "prayer," but in this context, a "place of prayer") and the synagogue as institutions that existed in the regions of Macedonia and Achaia (*Diaspora*, 110). Schnabel suggests that the expression in this context can also be translated "synagogue" (*Acts*, 679); see also Irina A. Levinskaya, *The Book of Acts in Its Diaspora Setting*, The Book of Acts in Its First Century Setting 5 (Grand Rapids: Eerdmans, 1996), 207–15. Luke might have a strong reason for his choice of terminology, but the functions of the prayer group and synagogue definitely overlap.

5. Anti-Semitism was prevalent in Roman society and there was antipathy toward "oriental religion that seemed to threaten the traditional gods and customs" (Witherington, *Acts*, 487).

letter to the Philippians, Paul also named two women who had actively served the community of believers, namely, Euodia and Syntyche (Phil 4:2–3). It is possible that they were among those who heard Paul preach during their Sabbath prayer meetings. It seems that there were a number of women who had been influential and had led the earliest Christian church in Philippi.

One of these, a woman named Lydia, who was herself a diasporan from Thyatira, was singled out for her generosity in hosting Paul (Acts 16:14). Presumably, Silas and Timothy enjoyed the same hospitality as well. The three missionaries were foreigners in Macedonia, and it was another diasporan who provided a home for them while they ministered there. Lydia hosted Paul and his team during their first visit to Macedonia. Schnabel observes

> The authenticity of Lydia's faith is indicated in her eagerness to provide hospitality to Paul and his coworkers . . . Lydia "invited" Paul and his missionary team to come into her house and stay there, for example, to sleep and eat in her house and to use it as the basis for their activities.[6]

Such treatment is the kind one offers to family members, and it is clear that Paul found a home with the household of Lydia while ministering at Philippi.[7] It is also possible that Lydia had later hosted the Philippian house church. The friendship she offered the trio was such that when Paul and Silas were released from prison, she was the one they first visited (16:40). Her hospitality and generosity seem to have influenced the other believers in Philippi so much that it became an important ethos of the Philippian congregation. The Philippian church's "partnership in the gospel" with Paul was consistent from the time he started his ministry there until the time he was imprisoned (Phil 1:5–7); this partnership included (but was not limited to) financial support (4:10–19). Their support for Paul and his ministry continued even as he ministered later in Thessalonica (1 Thess 4:16) and Corinth (2 Cor 11:9).

In contrast to the generosity and hospitality of the Philippian Christians, the owners of the clairvoyant girl responded with hostility against the missionaries. Paul's ministry in Philippi jeopardized the slave owners' source of

---

This explains why the Jews met outside the city. There also may not have been enough men to form a synagogue; hence, it was formed as a "prayer group" instead.

6. Schnabel, *Acts*, 681.

7. Jesus talking with the Samaritan woman raised some cultural sensitivities, as seen in the response of his disciples (John 4:27), but Lydia's hospitality was not considered scandalous at all. Keener points out that accepting hospitality from a woman could be acceptable if there were other people were involved who could prevent any misbehavior (*Acts*, 3:2229).

income.⁸ The slave girl had a spirit that enabled her to tell fortunes, and the owners capitalized on her ability so they could gain fortunes. The spirit at work in the clairvoyant girl was clearly different from the one who prohibited Paul from proceeding to Asia and led him to Macedonia (Acts 16:6–7). The same kind of challenge is experienced by contemporary Christian evangelists in Japan and South Korea.⁹

During the missionaries' stay in the city, the demon-possessed girl consistently provoked Paul. Eventually, he exorcized her, causing her to lose her supernatural ability to tell fortunes and causing her owners to lose the opportunity for financial gain (Acts 16:16–19). This led her owners to instigate an attack against Paul and his coworkers, accusing them of being Jews who caused disturbances to the city and who advocated customs unacceptable to the Romans (16:21).¹⁰ For the accusers to label Paul's team as Jews was technically inaccurate because Paul was the only diasporan Jew, Silas was a Gentile, and Timothy was a half-Jew who had probably spent his entire life among the Gentiles. Moreover, the accusers catalogued the actions of Paul, Silas, and Timothy. This is understandable because they needed a basis for bringing this case to the magistrates, but for them to link Paul's ethnicity to their actions reveals a kind of racial bias and stereotyping the local Philippians had against the diasporan Jews in the city. Their identification as "the Jews" could reflect a stereotyping of Jews as troublemakers,¹¹ which is comparable to the way Judeans looked at the Galileans, even fellow Jews from Galilee, as troublemakers or even insurgents (Luke 13:1–2; 23:6). The real issue was the economic loss of the slave owners, but the fact that they were able to get the Philippian magistrates and people on board with their plans by identifying the missionary trio as Jews who introduced unacceptable cultural practices showed their attitude toward the Jews as well. Identifying the missionaries as "Jews" could have been a description

---

8. Oracular consultations in temples cost significantly more than the average daily wage. David E. Aune, *Prophecy in Early Christianity and the Ancient Mediterranean World* (Grand Rapids: Eerdmans, 1983), 30. This explains the response of the masters of the slave girl.

9. See Kentaro Furusawa, "The Reception of Christianity in Okinawa: On Relations Between the Okinawa Baptist Convention and Native Religion," *Religion and Society* 13, no. 3 (2007): 284–302; David J. Kim, "Four Pillars and Four Diviners: Fate, Fluidity, and Invention in Horoscopic *Saju* Divination in Contemporary South Korea," *Journal of Korean Religions* 10, no. 2 (2019): 301–29.

10. Foreign religious practices could be a reason for persecution. This is still true, even until now, as Chee-Chiew Lee shows in "Responding to Persecution and Marginalization," in *Exploring the New Testament in Asia: An Evangelical Perspective*, ed. Samson L. Uytanlet and Bennet Lawrence (Carlisle: Langham Global Library, 2024), 211.

11. Schnabel, *Acts*, 686.

of the members of the Philippian church, which might have been composed mainly of diasporan Jews and with which the missionaries were associated, rather than the ethnicity of the three ministers. The local Philippians' hostility toward Paul, Silas, and Timothy might have been a reflection of their attitude toward the diasporan Jews who lived among them. As foreigners, it was natural for the trio to be unhomed among the natives of Philippi; being the cause of economic loss to some locals exacerbated their unhomedness.

Lydia will always be remembered for her hospitality and the slave owners for their hostility. Lydia's faith led her to give financially while the slave owners' financial loss all the more underscored their unbelief. Lydia provided a home for God's workers while the slave owners made them unhomed. The latter was the reason Paul and Silas were tortured and imprisoned (Acts 16:23–24). It is unclear why Timothy was not arrested with them. What is clear is that their "new house" could not provide them the comfort and convenience they experienced in the house of Lydia (16:24). Josephus described the Roman prison as "a gloomy dungeon" (*Jewish Antiquities* 19.7.1 §324), which provides us with a glimpse of the harsh condition of Paul and Silas.[12]

Suddenly, something supernatural occurred. An earthquake opened the prison doors and unfastened the bonds of the prisoners, including those of Paul and Silas (Acts 16:25–26). Not only were the prison doors opened, but an opportunity also opened for Paul to proclaim the gospel to the jailer, and the jailer opened his house for Paul and Silas (16:27–32). Moreover, that night, water was not only used to wash the wounds of Paul and Silas, it was also used to baptize the jailer and his family (16:33). It was not the responsibility of jailers to provide comfort and relief to prisoners, but to make sure they did not escape.[13] Not only did Paul and Silas become at-home with the jailer and his family, but more importantly, the jailer and his family became at-home with God.

At-Home with Thessalonian Believers, Unhomed with and Displaced by the Jewish Unbelievers of Thessalonica

After preaching at Philippi, Paul and his associates moved to the next city in the region of Macedonia. This is part of the so-called "Macedonian call." Upon

---

12. Schnabel, *Acts*, 535. Rapske details the horrible condition of prisoners of the empire, including their harsh physical environment, diet, and hygiene, among others. See *Paul in Roman Custody*, 195–225.

13. Bruce, *The Book of Acts*, 323.

arrival in the city, the first thing Paul did was visit the synagogue "as was [Paul's] custom" (Acts 17:2). The believers received Paul and Silas so warmly that the report about this spread to Macedonia and Achaia (1 Thess 1:8). The news reached Paul that Thessalonian believers had become an encouragement for believers from other cities including in how to make the missionaries at-home (1:9). Moreover, the Thessalonians' hospitality gave Paul and Silas comfort after their brutal experience in Philippi (2:1–2).

Like the Philippians, the Thessalonians also welcomed the missionaries. His experience as a missionary at Thessalonica was somewhat different to that at Philippi because Paul had to work while doing ministry at Thessalonica (2:9),[14] very likely to supplement the support the Philippians gave him (Phil 4:16). It seems that the congregation in Philippi was both able and willing to support the missionary:[15] the one in Thessalonica might have had the willingness but not the capability to do the same. It is even possible that Paul was the one helping some of the Thessalonians (1 Thess 2:7–8; cf. Acts 20:33–35). Idleness seems to have been an issue within the congregation (1 Thess 4:11; 5:12–14). This may have been aggravated by Paul's message about Christ's imminent return. Paul had to correct this misunderstanding and encourage them to work (2 Thess 3:6–12).

The message Paul preached to the Thessalonians focused on Christ's death and resurrection (Acts 17:3). They were also taught about the perils of idolatry, Christ's return, and future judgment (1 Thess 1:9–10). This explains the Thessalonians' questions about post-resurrection events, including Christ's return and God's promise of future salvation. A forged letter that claimed to have been from Paul was circulating, causing the Thessalonians alarm (2 Thess 2:2). The letter also claimed that the "day of the Lord" had already come. Paul had to assure them that it was not from him, that day was in the future, and when that day finally came, there will be those who will enjoy God's presence and those who will not (1:9). In other words, and to use Paul's own terminology of being "at-home with the Lord" (2 Cor 5:6, 8), there will be those who will be

---

14. Three weeks was too short for Paul to have received financial support from the Philippians a few times (Phil 4:15–16), to work (1 Thess 2:9; 2 Thess 3:7–8), and to be able to appoint elders before leaving (1 Thess 5:12). He could have stayed longer than three weeks in Thessalonica. The "three Sabbaths" mentioned in Acts 17:2 could refer to the period within which Paul reasoned with the unbelieving Jews in the synagogue, leading to his expulsion from the city (Keener, *Acts*, 3:2539–40).

15. There might have been some wealthy Philippians who gave generously. This does not mean that every member of the Macedonian church was affluent. Paul commended their generosity because they had given according to their means (2 Cor 8:1–3).

at-home eternally in God's presence, and by implication, there will be those who will be unhomed from God.

Paul's ministry in Thessalonica received positive responses from the members of the synagogue, including Jews and proselytes, and even some influential women in the city (Acts 17:4). Women of ancient Macedonia had a reputation for independence and entrepreneurship,[16] which explains the responses of those from Thessalonica and Philippi. For Paul to gain influence over these believers means that some Jewish Thessalonians would lose their influence over the believers.[17] No wonder it resulted in jealousy, which led them to take drastic actions by forming a mob, accusing Paul of insurrection, and attacking Jason, who was presumably the leader of the synagogue in Thessalonica (17:5–7). The Jewish Thessalonians' motivation was "political," involving both the government and the local community. First, it involved the government.[18] The message that Jesus is the Christ implies his kingship. Thus, the Jewish Thessalonians were partially correct when they brought this out in their accusation (17:7). However, they were incorrect to assume that the message was treasonous and a call to rebel against Caesar. It is understandable that the Jews were alarmed at this message. Given that the Jewish synagogue was where this message was initially propagated and there was no assurance that the Romans would be able to distinguish between believing and unbelieving Jews, the latter could well have suffered for the message believed by the former should the Romans have found out about this. Second, it involved the local community. As mentioned earlier, the influence of Paul over many of the Jewish Thessalonians meant that the influence of the unbelieving Jews would lessen. The accusation against Paul was so serious that Paul and Silas had to immediately leave the city (17:20) – once again, the missionaries were unhomed.

Paul and Silas were not the only ones who experienced rejection from the non-believing Thessalonian Jews. The local believers experienced the same kind of hostility: Paul compared their experience to that of the Judean Christians and the actions of the non-believing Jewish Thessalonians to those who participated in the death of Jesus and the prophets. So, Paul wrote, "For you,

---

16. Bruce, *The Book of Acts*, 323; W. W. Tarn and G. T. Griffith, *Hellenistic Civilisation*, rev. ed. (London: Meridian, 1952), 98–99.

17. Schnabel suggests that other reasons for jealousy could be the loss of influential patrons, and a loss of their rights and privileges in Roman society (*Acts*, 706).

18. Recent studies on the political implications of Christians being a minority in Southeast Asia include one by Daniel P. S. Goh and Terence Chong, "Ministering in the Middle: Christian Megachurches and Minoritarian Politics in Southeast Asia," *Politics and Religion* 15, no. 4 (2022): 722–41.

brothers, became imitators of the churches of God in Christ Jesus that are in Judea. For you suffered the same things from your own countrymen as they did from the Jews, who killed both the Lord Jesus and the prophets, and drove us out, and displease God and oppose all mankind" (1 Thess 2:14–15).

At-Home with the Berean Believers, Unhomed with and Displaced by the Jewish Unbelievers of Thessalonica (Again!)

With threats to their lives, Paul and Silas fled Thessalonica to another Macedonian city, Berea, where they met the Berean community of diasporan Jews. Berea was not along the Via Egnatia to the west, nor was it along the main highway to the south near the coastline; it was nearly fifty miles (seventy kilometers) southwest of Thessalonica. Travelling away from the main road might have been their reason for choosing to go to Berea,[19] unfortunately, their pursuers still caught up with them. It was clear to Paul that his assigned task was to bring the gospel message to the Gentiles (Greek, *ethnē*, or "nations"), however he had never forgotten the scattered Jews and made sure that they heard the gospel message. In one sense, the diasporan Jews were already part of the "nations" because of their geopolitical and sociocultural affiliations, but they remained Jews because of their ethnic origin. Paul would visit the synagogue whenever he arrived at a city where there was one and, as he did in other cities, Paul began his work in the Jewish synagogue of Berea (Acts 17:10).

Luke explicitly contrasted the Jews of Berea with those from Thessalonica, pointing out that the former "were more noble" (17:11). The word "noble" (Greek, *eugenēs*, literally "well-bred") can refer to someone of high-status, like members of a royal family.[20] In this context, however, being noble underscores an attitude of open-mindedness.[21] Thus, the Bereans being *eugenēs* was about having the right attitude, not about having the right pedigree, even though many of those who became believers were actually people of "high standing" (17:12). The Bereans' attitude was expressed in their "eagerness" to receive the word (17:11), which suggests that they did not listen with a *critical spirit or attitude*. This eagerness, followed with a "daily" examination of the Scriptures, shows that they listened with a *critical mind*. In contrast to the Bereans, the Thessalonians, although eager to accept Paul's teachings, were also eager to

---

19. Keener, *Acts*, 3:2561.

20. The Greek word *eugenēs* appears to be a combination of the adverb *eu* (well) and the noun *genos* (ancestral origin or family).

21. BDAG, s.v. *eugenēs*.

accept other teachings, which resulted in them being easily swayed as was demonstrated in their receiving of the forged letter that discussed the resurrection (2 Thess 2:2). The noble character of the Bereans was explicitly contrasted with the unguarded openness of the Thessalonians and implicitly with the overeagerness of the Athenians for new ideas, which Luke would later recount (Acts 17:19–21). With a critical mind and not a critical heart, the Bereans were ready to accept evidence. For them, maintaining an image of being theologically conservative was off the table, neither was associating with influential or powerful groups something to be considered. Their only concern was the truth, and they went where evidence from Scripture pointed them.

The Bereans' *eagerness to listen* to Paul was enough to make him at-home. Their cautiousness in accepting new and unfamiliar ideas was consistent with Paul's teaching principle because, while Paul was aware that he was teaching the truth with a good conscience, he never made himself the gold standard for teaching truth by claiming that truth is whatever he said it is. Paul was self-aware of his own limitations – he even warned the Galatians that if he taught anything other than the gospel, the Galatians must reject it (Gal 1:8–9). No wonder the Bereans' cautiousness was considered praiseworthy.

The Berean Christians were contrasted with the believers in Thessalonica in that the former had critical minds while the latter easily accepted new ideas, although both groups made Paul at-home. The Berean Christians were also contrasted with the non-believers in Thessalonica in that the former did not have critical spirits and the latter did, which was evident in their jealousy to the point that they attacked Paul in Thessalonica and pursued him to Berea, causing trouble for the missionaries once again (Acts 17:5, 13). Paul and Silas fled Berea[22] which led them to their first outreach in Greece.

At-Home with Athenian Philosophers and Believers, A Home for Believing Gentiles

From the region of Macedonia, Paul moved to the region of Achaia. The first city in Luke's account that Paul visited was Athens. Once again Paul entered the Jewish synagogue to persuade the Jews and the "devotees," presumably the proselytes who joined synagogue meetings (17:17). Paul did not just enter the synagogue to have discussions with Jews, he also went to the marketplace,

---

22. For the Bereans to accompany Paul to Greece showed a special kind of hospitality. They did not just take Paul to the ship, they made sure he arrived at his next stop safe (Keener, *Acts*, 3:2563).

where public philosophical discussions took place (17:17). His message centered around Jesus and the resurrection,[23] which the Epicureans and Stoics considered to be a message concerning "foreign divinities" (17:18).[24] Aside from the local philosophers, foreigners were also present in the marketplace, all eager to hear new ideas, and this opened an opportunity for Paul to continue speaking to them.

The last three episodes of Paul's mission in Acts 17 show three types of responses. First, the unbelieving Jews of Thessalonica refused to listen to unfamiliar ideas, especially if these "new ideas" threatened their power and influence over others. They responded in hostility to those who brought a message that loosened their grip on power. Second, the believing Jews of Berea were willing to listen to unfamiliar ideas but did so with caution. They responded with hospitality to those who brought evidence for the truth they preached. The third group were those who responded with openness to anyone, even those who brought new and unfamiliar ideas. The believing Thessalonians and Athenians fell under this category. There was, however, a crucial difference between these two groups. The Thessalonians did not seek new ideas but, when new ideas were presented to them, they passively accepted them. This made them hospitable and open to Paul, but it also made them vulnerable to false teachers. In contrast to the believing Thessalonians, the Athenians were seeking new ideas (17:21) and this also made them open to listening to Paul's teachings. In contrast to the unbelieving Thessalonians, the Athenians did not respond with violence against those with whom they disagreed. They might consider an idea ridiculous and risible (17:32), but not enough to zealously kill.

The first thing Paul observed about the city was the number of idols scattered within it. Pliny estimated that there were more than 73,000 statues in Athens (Pliny, *Natural History* 34.36),[25] presumably including both local and

---

23. The Athenians might have misunderstood Paul's message as a presentation of two gods named *Iēsous* and *Anastasis*, the Greek words for Jesus and resurrection. *Iēsous* also sounds like *Iasō* (Greek, "healing") and also the name of a daughter of Asklepios and the goddess of health. See Frederic Henry Chase, *The Credibility of the Books of Acts* (London: Macmillan, 1902), 205–6. Bruce also notes that the comment of the Athenians that Paul was a "preacher of foreign divinities recalls the charges brought at an earlier date in Athens against Protagoras, Anaxagoras, and Socrates (cf. Plato, *Euthyphro* 3B, *Apology* 24B–C; Xenophon, *Memorabilia* 1.1.1)." See Bruce, *The Book of Acts*, 330, n. 35.

24. While the two philosophic schools were lumped together in this account, it is likely that the group that levelled this accusation against Paul were the Epicureans, considering that the Stoics were more open to the existence of the gods, including foreign divinities. It is also important to note that while the Athenians were open to new ideas, they were not disposed to everything foreign (Keener, *Acts*, 3:2596–97).

25. Schnabel, *Acts*, 722.

foreign deities. Athens had become a home for all these gods, and the Athenians' hospitality was seen in their willingness to provide a space for the gods they might have inadvertently overlooked, so there was one altar dedicated "to the unknown god" (Acts 17:23).[26] The sight of it resulted in a strong emotion within Paul. The problem was not that Paul saw idols, but that he saw so many of them. They were so many that "the city *was full* of idols" (17:16, italics mine). As usual, he made sure to visit the diasporan Jews and proselytes in the city and welcomed everyone who was willing to listen to his message (17:17).

Luke described Paul's initial response upon seeing the images as being "provoked" (Greek, *paronthunō*), which can also be rendered "irritated," "annoyed," or "provoked to wrath."[27] None of these emotions naturally results in a welcoming posture. On the contrary, they can potentially lead to unwelcoming others, harmful acts, or even violence. Paul's irritation, however, did not cause him to leave the Athenians unhomed from the gospel. Rather, Paul's irritation led to a proclamation.

Paul's proclamation focused on the shared origin of both Jews and Gentiles – the creation. The creator God, "the Lord of heaven and earth . . . made from one man every nation of mankind to live on all the face of the earth, having determined allotted periods and the boundaries of their dwelling place, that they should seek God and perhaps feel their way toward him and find him" (17:24, 26–27). Bruce explains that part of the divine plan for creation was to provide an ideal home for humans.

> According to the Genesis account, the earth was formed and furnished to be a home for humanity before humanity itself was brought into being to occupy it; the tenses of the Greek verbs here similarly suggest that "the determination of man's home preceded his creation, in the divine plan." And part of the forming and furnishing of this home consisted in the regulation of the "allotted seasons," by which, after the analogy of the Lystran speech (14:17), we are probably to understand the seasons of the year by whose sequence annual provision is made for the supply of food.[28]

---

26. Religious pluralism was clearly one major challenge for Christian missionaries in ancient Athens. The same problem is prevalent in Asia. The situation in Africa is no different. See Tokunboh Adeyemo, "Religious Pluralism," *Africa Bible Commentary*, ed. Tokunboh Adeyemo (Carlisle: HippoBooks, 2006), 1558.

27. BDAG, s.v. *eugenēs*.

28. Bruce, *The Book of Acts*, 334.

Humans rejected this home offered by the creator God, and instead of seeking him, humans turned to the created gods, those that have been fashioned by human hands. This continuous rejection of God by humanity began with that of Adam and Eve, the consequence of which was being driven away from their original home, the garden of Eden. In some sense, they were "unhomed," and consequently, the rest of humanity was as well.

Paul's message to the Athenians at the Areopagus (which was composed of many Greek philosophers) and his message to the diasporan Jews at Antioch are also worth a comparison. Paul addressed the Jews of Antioch as "men of Israel" and "those who fear God" (13:16), and the Athenians as "men of Athens" and those who are "religious" (17:22) – in both cases, highlighting the audiences' devotion to a deity. While speaking to the Jews, Paul referred to God as "God of this people Israel" (13:17) and referred to their common ancestry as "our fathers" (13:17). While speaking to Gentiles, Paul referred to God as the "God who made the world," the "Lord of heaven and earth," and one that is not made by man (17:23–24); he then acknowledged that they shared a common ancestry to the "one man" (17:26). In reviewing history, Paul traced the Jews' story from Exodus until Jesus (13:17–19), but to the Athenians, he went as far back as the story of creation (17:26–27). Paul also cited authorities in his message: to the Jews, he quoted the Scripture (13:33–38) and, to the Greeks, he cited their philosophers (17:28).[29] The story of the resurrection was shared with both groups (13:30–34; 17:31–32). To the Jews, he highlighted their freedom from the things that the law was unable to free them from (13:38–39), but he reminded both groups about the coming divine judgment (13:40–41; 17:30–31). The core of Paul's message was the same for both groups, but his presentation of the gospel to the two groups varied. This could be a lesson on methods of evangelism. More importantly, Paul's messages showed both groups how they could be truly at-home with God with forgiveness and freedom (13:38–39), eternal life for those who believe (13:47–48), and divine assurance for those who repent (17:30–31).

---

29. Paul's quotation from Greek philosophers suggests he acknowledged that the writing was deemed authoritative by the listeners and that it contained some truths with which he could agree. Quotation does not imply endorsement of the writing as Scripture. As Bruce explains, "the direct quotations from pagan poets have their place as points of contact with the hearers and illustrate the argument in terms familiar to them, but they in no way commit the speaker to acquiescence in their philosophical presuppositions" (*The Book of Acts*, 358).

Unhomed with Jewish Corinthian Unbelievers, Unhomed Even with Some Corinthian Believers

From Athens, Paul moved to another city in Achaia, Corinth, where he frequented the synagogue, speaking to Jews and Greeks, presumably proselytes (Acts 18:1, 4). While at Corinth, Paul stayed with a Jewish Italian couple, Priscilla and Aquila (18:2). When Claudius became emperor he expelled the Jews from Rome,[30] including this couple, making them unhomed (18:2). They moved to Achaia where they made tents for a living. Corinth was one of the cities where travelling philosophers like the Sophists stopped to make a living by giving rhetorical discourses. One possible reason Paul made sure he was financially independent from the church was to avoid being identified with these teachers.[31] Paul shared the same trade with Priscilla and Aquila, so he stayed with the couple and worked with them. The couple were also diasporan Jews who became believers in Christ. It is unclear whether they became believers as a result of Paul's ministry. There were diasporan Jews from Rome who heard Peter preach the gospel on the first Pentecost after the resurrection (2:10). It is possible that the couple themselves were in Jerusalem on Pentecost and believed the gospel, or they heard the gospel from Jewish Romans who believed in Christ as a result of Peter's sermon and went back to Rome to proclaim the message. There is no solid evidence for Priscilla and Aquila already being Christians but, if this was the case, it means that Paul did not start his work at Corinth from scratch because there were already witnesses there before Paul arrived.

Paul's ministry among the Jews was not met with enthusiasm. His rejection by Jewish Corinthians led Paul to focus his work away from the diasporan Jews there (18:6b). There were still diasporan Jews in Corinth who believed and were baptized (18:7–8), but the group "many of the Corinthians" who believed and were baptized were presumably local Gentiles (18:8). Like the unbelieving Jews of Thessalonica, the unbelieving Jews of Corinth responded to Paul with hostility. Unlike his experiences in Macedonia, wherein Paul endured both verbal and physical abuses for preaching the gospel, there had been no threat to his life thus far in Achaia, but Paul was not spared from being verbally abused (18:6a). This did not make Paul's life more bearable at Corinth; it was not just the unbelievers who were hostile toward Paul but even the believers as well.

---

30. For a more detailed discussion on the expulsion of the Jews during the reign of Claudius, see Foakes-Jackson and Lake, *Beginnings of Christianity*, 5:459–60.

31. Witherington, *Acts*, 547–48.

Luke described the hostility of the diasporan Jews in Corinth as a "united attack"; they went to great lengths to oppose Paul even taking him to the Corinthian tribunal, accusing him of disrespecting the Mosaic law (18:12–13). Resident alien communities were given rights either to settle disputes like this among themselves or to bring charges before the proconsul.[32] The Jewish Corinthians chose the latter option. The indifference shown by the proconsul of Achaia is not commendable at all; though it definitely worked in Paul's favor (18:13–15), it led to Sosthenes, the leader of the synagogue, being beaten before Gallio, presumably in an unsuccessful attempt to sway the proconsul to change his decision in their favor (18:17).[33]

Paul's two surviving letters to the Corinthian Christians show that the hostility Paul endured at Corinth came not only from the Jewish unbelievers but also from the believers. It is understandable that unbelievers could be hostile toward Paul, but here, even believers were treating him in the same way. It is not surprising then that the description Paul used to describe such believers was "carnal" or "of the flesh" (1 Cor 3:1–3). This means that, while ministering at Corinth, the hostility Paul experienced was on two fronts: from the unbelieving Jews and from many believers within the congregation. In short, Paul was twice unhomed at Corinth. It was during this period that Paul received another instruction from the Lord, the second time the Lord spoke to Paul in Luke's account (the first one being Paul's calling to ministry in Acts 9:1–18). With the kind of rejection Paul experienced from both unbelievers and believers at Corinth, the Lord encouraged Paul by reminding him that there were still many in Corinth who belonged to him, "Do not be afraid, but go on speaking and do not be silent, for I am with you, and no one will attack you to harm you, for I have many in this city who are my people" (18:9–10). These words are reminiscent of the Lord's encouragement to Elijah when Jezebel was seeking to kill him and he had to flee (1 Kgs 19:18). There remained a group of people who would receive Elijah's message, and this was enough for him to keep going despite being displaced by the queen seeking his life. In the same way, for Paul, there remained a group of people who would receive his message despite the rejection of the Jewish unbelievers and many Corinthian believers. It was with this group that Paul could be at-home while being unhomed with the two aforementioned groups.

---

32. Bruce W. Winter, *After Paul Left Corinth: The Influence of Secular Ethics and Social Change* (Grand Rapids: Eerdmans, 2001), 295.

33. For a more detailed discussion on the identity of Sergius Paulus, see Foakes-Jackson and Lake, *Beginnings of Christianity*, 5:460–64.

Aside from Silas and Timothy, who arrived at Corinth later than Paul (Acts 18:5), and Priscilla and Aquila, who hosted Paul and later became mentors to Apollos (18:24–28), Luke mentioned several believers with whom Paul found encouragement while ministering at Corinth. Titius Justus, Crispus (who was a synagogue ruler), and his family were some of the early members of the Corinthian congregation (18:7–8). There was also Sosthenes, the earlier mentioned ruler of the synagogue who was beaten before Gallio for welcoming Paul (18:17) and who was with Paul when he wrote his first letter (1 Cor 1:1).

Paul's surviving letters provide additional information, allowing us to get a broader and clearer picture of the kind of challenges he faced with the Christians of Corinth. Clues from these two letters tick several boxes on textbook checklists for narcissism,[34] except that Paul was not dealing with an individual but a religious community with a subgroup embodying these traits.[35]

First, hints from Paul's letters suggest that he was dealing with a community with members who had a strong sense of self-importance.[36] There are several ways that this was expressed by many of the Christians in Corinth. The schism within the community was a result of members wanting to associate themselves with leaders they deemed superior over others so Paul used himself, Apollos, and Peter as representative leaders of the various factions (1 Cor 1:11–13; 3:1–23; 4:16). A group led by a certain Chloe could be one of

---

34. Nine qualities were listed by the American Psychiatric Association as diagnostic criteria for Narcissistic Personality Disorder (NPD), and we are using this as a list of traits that may indicate narcissistic tendencies: (1) grandiosity; (2) fantasy of unlimited success, power, brilliance, beauty, and ideal love; (3) belief that they are special, so they associate with people perceived as special or those of high status; (4) need for excessive admiration; (5) sense of entitlement and unreasonable expectation; (6) exploitative; (7) lacking empathy; (8) envious of others and believe others are envious of them; and (9) arrogant or haughty behavior. See Glen O. Gabbard and Holly Crisp, *Narcissism and Its Discontents: Diagnostic Dilemmas and Treatment Strategies with Narcissistic Patients* (Washington, DC: American Psychiatric Association Publishing, 2018), 7. Gabbard and Crisp warn about oversimplifying diagnosis (see page 8). However, the purpose of listing this here is not to perform a diagnosis. The author of this current work is not a trained psychiatrist, and thus, is *unqualified* to make any *individual* psychiatric diagnosis. However, the connections between characteristics in APA's list and the clues hinted in Paul's two letters to the community are just too stark to ignore. The discussion that follows, however, is based on literary observations of the biblical text and an attempt to show how these narcissistic traits manifest in a *community*.

35. The list of diagnostic criteria in the previous footnote is for individuals. These traits are not limited to individuals, however. Psychiatrists recognize parallels between individuals and communities in what they call "collective narcissism." See Agnieszka Golec de Zavala, Karolina Dyduch-Hazar, and Dorottya Lantos, "Collective Narcissism: Political Consequences of Investing Self-Worth in the Ingroup's Image," *Advances in Political Psychology* 40, supp. 1 (2019): 38.

36. This checks items 1 & 3.

these groups (1:11).³⁷ Associating with one leader resulted in unnecessarily rejecting and downplaying the contribution of the others. The battle was not between truth and error, but about which leader had more to show so the followers could glory in being associated with this influential figure, because the more prominent the leader, the more bragging rights the followers had for the association.

Second, some members showed a sense of grandiosity; this can be seen not only in their association with important individuals, but also in their propensity to boast.³⁸ In the Greek New Testament (Nestle Aland 28th edition), the words *kauchaomai* (verb, "to boast"), *kauchēma* (noun, "boast" or "boastful words"), and *kauchēsis* (noun, "boast" or "act of boasting") occur thirty-seven, eleven, and eleven times, respectively. These same words occur respectively in the two Corinthian correspondences twenty-six, six, and seven times. This means that Paul used these three words a total of thirty-nine times in his two letters to the Corinthians, which is almost two-thirds of the fifty-nine total occurrences of these words in the entire NT. One can infer, then, that boasting was a serious problem within the Corinthian Christian community. Boasting is a good way for people to announce their superiority over others, whether through explicitly grand claims or through humble bragging. It can be a way to fill one's need for validation. Paul acknowledged that a few of the Corinthians were wise, noble, and mighty by the world's standards (1 Cor 1:26–27), but the community's overall self-perception was one that required the apostle to remind them to put their feet back on the ground (4:7). While ministering in the community, Paul was often the subject of evaluation and critique by some members (4:3) and was often slandered for not meeting their "standards" (4:13). Some members did not have any qualms about showing their disrespect toward the apostle, whether through their reluctant or resentful financial support (9:1–18) that requires the recipients of help to lose their dignity, or their open criticism of the apostle (2:1–5; 2 Cor 10:1–2).

Aside from associating themselves with great people and boasting about themselves, a third way they demonstrated their sense of self-importance

---

37. The Greek expression *tōn Chloēs* ("those that belonged to Chloe") in 1 Cor 1:11 is similar to the expressions *Paulou* ("person belonging to Paul") and *Apollō* ("person belonging to Apollos") in 1:12, and this may be a hint that there was a faction led by this female leader, Chloe (1:11–12). Her "people" need not be seen as Paul's "eyes and ears" in Corinth, which he appointed as informants or tattletales to spy for him. It is more likely that the "people of Chloe" were one faction in the community that was either trying to find a solution to the issue or trying to get the support of the apostle. What is clear is that Paul did take sides.

38. This checks item 9.

was in how they treated others who they deemed less than them.[39] Certain spiritual gifts were celebrated while others were frowned upon: Paul had to remind them of the importance of every kind of spiritual gift and the value of every work done for building up the one body of Christ (1 Cor 12:1–31). The eloquence of Apollos worked to his advantage. After his brief ministry at Ephesus and training with Priscilla and Aquila, he went to Corinth in Achaia (Acts 18:24–19:1), and many Corinthians were drawn to him because of his abilities. This attitude of self-importance was not only seen in the way they treated other members within the community; it was seen even in the way they treated Paul, whose appearance and eloquence (or lack of) were condescended to (2 Cor 10:10; 11:6) and whose apostolic authority was questioned (11:1–12:21). The Corinthian believers who looked down on Paul were not shy in expressing their disdain (10:10). But, apparently, they did not treat everyone the same way. Paul had to go through much inhospitality that many of his contemporaries did not endure.

Despite their giftedness, Paul revealed that envy was a serious issue among the Corinthians, which was one of the reasons for their divisiveness.[40] This checks the fourth box. Their carnality was expressed as "envy and strife" (1 Cor 3:3), so Paul had to underscore love's expression as not being envious (13:4). Envy is an issue of the heart, and this could be what motivated them to make an exaggerated assessment of themselves (4:7).

Fifth, the Corinthians' lack of moral compass ticks another box in the checklist.[41] Paul described the sin committed as something that would not pass any moral standards, even the ones held by Gentiles (5:1). The Jews held a high moral standard when it came to sexual relations (see Lev 18:1–30), which is what separated them from the nations. Paul's statement need not be considered a slight against non-Jews, but another way of saying that their immoral acts would not be acceptable by any moral standards. Yet the response of the congregation was one of haughty indifference, as though the sin committed was a trivial matter. Hence Paul rebuked them, "You have become arrogant and

---

39. This checks item 3 and, to a certain extent, item 7.

40. This checks item 8 and, to some extent, item 3.

41. A lack of moral standard might reflect a sense of entitlement or the expectation that they were exempt from any standard, checking item 5. Ancient writers attested to the moral depravity of the Corinthians, but this could be an exaggeration as part of the Athenians propaganda against a rival city than an accurate reflection of the Corinthian lifestyle (Bruce, *The Book of Acts*, 345; Schnabel, *Acts*, 755). Nonetheless, Paul had to deal with a community that was, to a large extent, tolerant of such a lifestyle among its members.

have not mourned" (1 Cor 5:2). No wonder they did not consider disciplinary action a necessity!

Sixth, in conjunction with the lack of moral compass was a lack of guilt and shame, checking yet another box.[42] This was one of the problems that was resolved after the first letter so Paul had to reassure them in his second letter that genuine sorrow for sins could lead to repentance (2 Cor 7:8–12) and that forgiveness should be offered to the repentant (2:1–11).

Seventh, with their apparent lack of empathy, especially toward the poor members of the congregation, another box was checked.[43] Earlier, we saw how some factions within the congregation were based on their affiliations with influential leaders and other factions were based on the individual's talents and abilities. Another factor that created factions was the member's social status – this was particularly obvious whenever they celebrated the Lord's Supper (1 Cor 11:18–21). The church was segregated based on social standing. This was not praiseworthy to say the least (11:22); the result of the discrimination was that the Lord's table was desecrated or, to use Paul's words, the bread and the cup were received in an "unworthy manner" (11:27). The Corinthians were not consistently condescending toward those in the lower social standing.[44] Paul commended them for their generosity toward the believers in Jerusalem (2 Cor 9:1–15), which was comparable to that of the Macedonians who were earlier commended by Paul (8:1–5). To be compared to the Macedonians in terms of generosity can be considered high praise. Ironically, while the Corinthians could express their generosity toward believers in another region, they seemed unable to show the same kind of generosity to those within their own congregation.

Paul did not only have to deal with the unbelieving Jews at Corinth – the believers with an attitude of superiority also posed a challenge for him. It should not be surprising that unbelievers rejected him nor that the disrespect he received from the believers added extra pressure. No wonder Paul preferred not to receive any financial support from the Corinthian congregation as he

---

42. The inability to feel remorse for their wrongdoings might reflect an attitude similar to the ones exhibited by their lack of moral standard, thus checking item 5. It can also reflect a lack of empathy.

43. This checks item 7.

44. The problem caused by the economic disparity among the members was not just a problem of the first-century Corinthian church. It remains a challenge even now. See Julio de Santa Ana, "Mission of the Church in a World Torn Between Poor and Rich," *International Review of Mission* 72, no. 1 (1983): 20–31.

ministered to them.⁴⁵ His source of income as he ministered at Corinth was tentmaking and support from the Philippians. Paul ministered at Corinth for a year and a half (Acts 18:11). The length of his stay in the region of Achaia testifies, to some extent, to his resilience in ministry. He was not able to stay long in the other cities he previously visited, mainly because there were threats to his life, nonetheless, Paul's lengthier stay at Corinth was far from ideal, especially because the difficulties he faced in ministry were not brought about by non-believers, but by the "saints in Corinth."

Visiting Home Church at Antioch and "Home Churches" in Galatia, At-Home with John the Baptizer's Disciples, Unhomed Among the Craftsmen at Ephesus

After ministering a few years in the regions of Macedonia and Achaia, there remained unfinished business as far as Paul's earlier plan was concerned. His plan to visit Asia was halted, having been "forbidden by the Holy Spirit" twice (Acts 16:6–7). After his work in Achaia, he was ready to visit his home church in Antioch of Syria (18:18), but he passed through Asia briefly. Upon arriving at Ephesus of Asia, as he would normally do, he visited the synagogue to persuade the Jews of the gospel (18:19).

The members of the Ephesian synagogue welcomed him and wanted him to stay (18:20), but he refused. Nonetheless, he promised to return "if God wills" (18:21). Paul clearly learned from his first attempt to visit Asia that God *may* forbid even his servants to fulfil their plans if they are not according to his will (16:6–7). Having been away from his sending church for quite some time, Paul might have felt obliged to bring them a report about his ministry, similar to that after his earlier ministry in Galatia and Phrygia (14:26–28). Not much was said about his visit to his home church, except that he soon went to visit the churches in Galatia and Phrygia "strengthening the disciples" (18:23). This visit did not record hostile experiences from the non-believing residents of these regions. This does not necessarily mean that the hostility was spent, nonetheless, the hospitality shown to him by the disciples is evidence that Paul found a home among the people to whom he ministered.

---

45. For a fuller discussion on the reasons and the dynamics that resulted in this arrangement, see Samson L. Uytanlet, "Tentmaking: Paul's Missionary Strategy?," *Evangelical Mission Quarterly* 59, no. 1 (2023): 53–55. In addition, it was considered improper for rabbis of Judaism to receive payment for teaching, so most of them practiced some form of trade (Bruce, *The Book of Acts*, 346).

As a Jew from Tarsus, he must have experienced some degree of foreignness, whether as a Jew in a land of the Gentiles, or even as he visited Jerusalem, being a diasporan in the land of the Jews. It is possible that with his education and trade, Paul found a home among the Tarsians, and with his commitment to the Mosaic law and as a Pharisee, he became prominent, especially within the religious community. With the influence of Barnabas, Paul also became a prominent leader of the church in Antioch of Syria, where he found "home." With the hospitality of the churches in Galatia and Phrygia, Paul, the diasporan Jew, found many other "homes" in these regions.

The region of Asia was one that Paul wanted to ensure he visited on his way westward. His desire was to travel to the regions further west, as far as Illyricum (Rom 15:19–20). Paul kept his promise of going back to Ephesus, where he found a home among the disciples of John the Baptizer, encountered the seven sons of Sceva, and faced the angry craftsmen and occult practitioners.

Twelve followers of John the Baptizer were the first group of believers Paul encountered upon his return to Ephesus (Acts 19:4, 7). There is no record of how they heard John's message. Although it is possible that they visited Galilee more than a decade earlier while John was still preaching publicly,[46] a more plausible scenario is that one of John's disciples had been preaching itinerantly like Paul and that this disciple reached as far as Asia Minor. As a result, aside from these twelve men, others had also received the message – including Apollos who "spoke and taught accurately the things concerning Jesus, though he knew only the baptism of John" (18:25). Paul was clearly recalling John's endorsement of Jesus with his statement, "John baptized with the baptism of repentance, telling the people to believe in the one who was to come after him, that is, Jesus" (19:4; cf. Matt 3:11; Mark 1:7; John 1:15–30). Having been baptized by John, these twelve men must have heard the message of repentance and of God's kingdom, a belief to which they had clearly held faithfully for many years. While it conveyed the same message that Jesus also proclaimed, it was, at best, incomplete because it did not include the message concerning Christ's death and resurrection (cf. 1 Cor 15:14). So, Paul had to update them about a more recent development so that they, too, were baptized "in the name of the Lord Jesus" (Acts 19:5).

The religious identities of these twelve men prior to their baptism in the name of Christ remains unclear. They cannot have claimed to be Christians because they did not yet know Christ; therefore they cannot have been legiti-

---

46. These men were not direct "disciples" of John because, if they were, Luke could have simply indicated it. But they were "followers" (Bruce, *The Book of Acts*, 383).

mately acknowledged as disciples of Jesus. For this reason, they were unhomed in relation to the universal Christian community. With Paul introducing Jesus and his message to them, and having been baptized in his name, the twelve Ephesians were officially welcomed into the universal body of Christ. The same can be said about the other members of the Ephesian synagogue who heard messages about the kingdom of God in the three months that followed (19:8).

Similar to earlier events in Samaria, where Peter personally witnessed the outpouring of the Spirit upon those baptized in the name of Jesus (8:14–18), Paul witnessed the same among the Ephesians (19:6). In both cases, the Spirit manifested through the believers who spoke in tongues. Moreover, there were apostles who witnessed these manifestations as confirmation that both the Samaritan and Ephesian believers were part of the same body, along with those in Jerusalem. If these three incidents (the Spirit's manifestation in Jerusalem, in Samaria, and in Ephesus) had not occurred, the universal church would have been immediately divided, even before the local churches recognized they belonged to the same body of Christ. The similar manifestations underscored the fact that the same Spirit worked through all these communities, therefore, they were part of one and the same larger body. Through the Spirit's manifestations, those outside Judea, whether Samaritans, diasporan Jews, or Gentiles, could also be at-home within the universal Church of Christ and with the Jewish believers in Jerusalem.

Paul's experience at Ephesus, as in the places he previously visited, was a mixture of hospitality and rejection. While some members of the synagogue at Ephesus welcomed his message about the kingdom in the same way they accepted John the Baptizer's message about the same, others maligned "the Way" (19:9).[47] For this reason, Paul had to meet with the disciples in another venue, the hall of Tyrannus, which was a more neutral venue for Paul to continue preaching. This location allowed him to minister in the next two years even to those who were not joining the synagogue, so that many Jews and Greeks in the region of Asia learned how they could be at-home with the Lord (19:9–10). Paul's move from the synagogue to another venue caused some of the members of the synagogue to leave, and those who left may have

---

47. John the Baptizer was known as the one who prepared "the way" (Matt 3:3; Mark 1:3; Luke 3:4; John 1:23). Jesus also claimed to be "the Way" (John 14:6) and to have taught "the way" of God (Luke 20:21; cf. Acts 18:25–26). By the time of the book of Acts, the expression had become a name to refer to the followers of Jesus (Acts 9:2; 19:9, 23; 24:14, 22), perhaps even being used initially as a derogatory description by critics.

even been relatives of those who were left behind, which inevitably resulted in increased hostility.[48]

Aside from teaching regularly in the school of Tyrannus, Paul also healed the sick and performed exorcisms (presumably within the said two-year period) (19:11–12). Luke recounted how handkerchiefs and aprons were used for healing in this city; these items were brought by the devotees and used to touch Paul, not things distributed by Paul or his associates.[49] This suggests that the use of these items reflected the people's misunderstanding of Paul's healing,[50] which is similar to the bleeding woman's false assumption, "If I touch even his garments, I will be made well" (Mark 5:28). Their faith, despite being accompanied by false assumptions, was honored by God, and they were made well. Luke made it clear that it was God who "was doing extraordinary miracles by the hands of Paul" (Acts 19:11). Clues from Paul's letter to the Ephesians, such as his greetings wherein he implied conflict in the "heavenly realms" (Eph 1:3, 19–23) and his extended discussions on spiritual battle (6:10–20), suggest that the Ephesians were very much involved in these things. Luke's account of Paul's ministry in Ephesus confirms that the residents were consciously and actively involved in spiritual battle. First, Luke's description gives the impression that Paul performed multiple exorcisms within the two-year period he was at Ephesus (Acts 19:12). Second, Paul was not the only one performing exorcism – there were itinerant exorcists, the seven sons of Sceva, going around exorcizing.

There are a couple of questions to consider here. How often can one encounter a demon-possessed person in a city with only about 200,000 inhabitants?[51] What created the need for exorcists to be itinerant? Luke's account suggests that there had been numerous cases of demon possession in this city at that period, and he gave a clue why this was so.

> And many of those who were now believers came, confessing and divulging their practices. And a number of those who had prac-

---

48. Keener, *Acts*, 3:2825–26.

49. Even now, the belief that healing power can be transmitted from a "divine healer" to a sick person is prevalent in places like Hawaii (see Wende Elizabeth Marshall, *Potent Mana: Lessons in Power in Healing*, UPCC Book Collections on Project MUSE [Albany: SUNY Press, 2011]), in New Zealand and Australia (see Wiremu NiaNia, "Restoring Mana and Taking Care of Wairua: A Story of Māori Whānau Healing," *Australian & New Zealand Journal of Family Therapy* 38, no. 1 [2017]: 72–97), and even among the devotees of the Black Nazarene in the Philippines.

50. The Ephesians might have viewed handkerchiefs and aprons as some kind of talisman or amulets, reflecting their traditional views about magic (Schnabel, *Acts*, 390).

51. Schnabel, *Acts*, 783.

tised magic arts brought their books together and burned them in the sight of all. And they counted the value of them and found it came to fifty thousand pieces of silver." (19:18–19)

The residents were so deeply involved in occultism that they were willing collectively to spend a staggering amount of money for the practice.[52] Luke depicted a community of former occult practitioners who were willing to suffer economic losses for the sake of finding a new home with other believers in God's kingdom.

In contrast to the community of former occult practitioners was the guild of silversmiths and craftsmen of Artemis. The former used their silver to buy materials for witchcraft; the latter used silver for making shrines. The former voluntarily suffered loss to follow Christ, but the latter safeguarded their interest by instigating a riot against the herald of Christ. One of the silversmiths, Demetrius, led the craftsmen in their opposition against Paul. Demetrius candidly admitted

> Men, you know that *from this business we have our wealth*. And you see and hear that not only in Ephesus but in almost all of Asia this Paul has persuaded and turned away a great many people, saying that gods made with hands are not gods. And *there is danger* not only that this *trade* of ours may come into disrepute but also that the temple of the great goddess Artemis may be counted as nothing, and that she may even be deposed from her magnificence, she whom all Asia and the world worship. (19:25–27, italics mine)

Like the owner of the clairvoyant slave girl, the businesses of Demetrius and other craftsmen were in jeopardy because of the new-found faith of the Ephesians. In addition, the honor of their goddess was also now in question. At this period, Ephesus was at a religious and cultural crossroads, for while the city remained the center of worship for the Greek hunter-goddess, Artemis, the wealthy Ephesians were beginning to fund the construction of temples and statues honoring Roman deities.[53] Paul entering the city and introducing the

---

52. If we simply assume that a piece of silver is equivalent to their daily wage, fifty thousand pieces of silver is equivalent to almost one hundred and thirty-seven years of work without a break. The amount was assessed only for those who surrendered their collections, which presumably was just a small fraction of the total number of occult practitioners.

53. Christine M. Thomas, "At Home in the City of Artemis: Religion in Ephesos in the Literary Imagination of the Roman Period," in *Ephesos, Metropolis of Asia: An Interdisciplinary Approach to Its Archaeology, Religion, and Culture*, ed. Helmut Koester. Harvard Theological

God known only to a small and perhaps insignificant sector of society might not have been the main problem, but the devotees did not consider it a small matter for Paul's message to consequently affect the loyalty of the locals toward their patron deity. This issue seems to have been of greater concern for the devotees of Artemis than for the craftsmen, who had been profiting from the religious piety of the devotees, but the concern was enough to stir up the crowd and partially mask their primary concern, which was their reducing sales and profits.[54] Chaos ensued; importantly, as Luke pointed out, the crowd of accusers were not in agreement with each other as to why they were gathered and why they were against Paul (19:32). The only thing that settled them down was the fear of being charged by the Romans for rioting (19:40). Paul was unharmed by the Ephesian rioters, which was likely what he was referencing when he recalled how he fought the "beasts at Ephesus" (1 Cor 15:32). The incident was enough to signal to Paul that it was time to leave (Acts 20:1). Once again, the apostle was unhomed.

At-Home with the Ephesian Believers, Comforting Those Left at Home

Paul ministered in Asia for two years (Acts 19:10). This period may not seem long but, for an itinerant missionary like Paul, it is a significant amount of time. According to Luke's account, this was the longest he stayed in one region, exceeding his eighteen-month stay in Achaia (18:11). His two-year stay in Asia was more than enough for Paul to develop a close bond with the Christians in Ephesus. After the riot at Ephesus, Paul was forced to leave (19:21–20:1), but he made sure to encourage the Ephesians before departing for Greece (20:2). His plan was to go to Jerusalem for Pentecost (20:6, 16), so he only stayed in Greece for three months (20:3) and a week in Troas (20:6) before leaving again. On his way to Jerusalem, he visited the Ephesians.

Paul's stay at Ephesus was characterized by mutual hospitality and encouragement. Before leaving Ephesus for Greece the first time, Paul "had given them

---

Studies 41 (Valley Forge: Trinity, 1995), 81–117.

54. Craftsmen were not considered as having high-status in ancient Roman societies, but the economic status of a person could be different from their social status (Keener, *Acts*, 3:2880–81). As craftsmen, they used their skills to earn a living, and considering that their products met the religious needs of the people, the business of Demetrius and his colleagues must have been thriving.

much encouragement" (20:2); and after raising Eutychus to life,[55] the Ephesians "were not a little comforted" (20:12). Paul had to leave this temporary home permanently – as he predicted, "they would never see his face again" (20:38).

Social Status and Being Unhomed

While racial and ethnic tensions existed between the Jews and the Gentiles, the willingness of Jews to welcome and accommodate people of other races was greater than we are often willing to give them credit for. The same can be said about Gentiles accommodating Jews in diaspora. One area where this accommodation is evident is intermarriage, as seen in the case of Timothy's parents. While his Jewish maternal side of the family retained some Jewish cultural distinctives, Luke presented Timothy as a disciple from Lystra (Acts 16:1). Similarly, when Paul arrived in the region as a missionary, both the Jewish Lycaonians and the natives made him feel at-home among them. Paul repeatedly spoke against certain moral and cultural practices of these people when these practices were against God's standard, but he never spoke of the superiority of any ethnicity or race.

As a missionary, Paul posed no threat to the ethnic identities of the Gentiles to whom he preached the gospel. The same cannot be said about the financial status of some of Paul's audience. Paul's encounters with the clairvoyant slave girl (16:16–24) and with the devotees of Artemis in Ephesus (19:24–27) were victorious; through his message, God delivered both the girl and the devotees from spiritual bondage. On the other hand, Paul's "victory" resulted in financial losses for the owners of the slave girl and the craftsmen who were profiting from the Ephesian worshippers' devotion to their goddess. With their financial losses came a diminished status in society, prompting them to assert their power and influence in order to regain their former standing. These two incidents resulted in Paul's imprisonment in Philippi (16:24) and a threat to Paul's life in Ephesus (19:28–41). In these same cities, there were those who gave up a significant portion of their wealth, but there is no hint in the narrative that they saw Paul as a threat to their status and influence in society. At Philippi, Lydia offered hospitality to Paul and provided for his needs (16:14–15) although, even in her generosity, she felt unworthy to give to the Lord's work

---

55. For a discussion on the significance of this episode on the death and resurrection of Eutychus, see Eric C. Smith, "The Fall and Rise of Eutychus: The Church of Paul and the Spatial Habitus of Luke," *Biblical Interpretation* 28, no. 2 (2020): 228–45; David H. Wenkel, "The Primacy of Preaching in the Resurrection of Eutychus in Acts 20:7–12," *Biblische Notizen* 197 (2023): 95–110.

(16:15). At Ephesus, many occult practitioners also surrendered their occult books to the fire because of their newfound commitment to Jesus (19:18–20).

With wealth comes power. In contrast to Lydia, who considered it an honor to be able to show hospitality to Paul and did not use her generosity as an opportunity to gain power over the apostle, some Corinthian believers considered their financial capabilities placed themselves above others. The Philippians supported Paul without expecting anything in return. The situation seems to have been different in Corinth, so Paul refused to accept their support. Aside from their financial status, some Corinthians also perceived themselves as having superior abilities, which entitled them to look down on others.

Paul's message about the kingship of Christ also jeopardized the political standing of the unbelieving Jews in Thessalonica. For this reason, they reaffirmed their loyalty to the emperor by making it clear they disagreed with Paul's messages that opposed the decrees of Caesar and presented Jesus as king (17:7). The proclamation of Jesus as king could easily have been interpreted as subversive which would have endangered not only the Jewish Christians but also the non-believing Jews at Thessalonica. The latter could not afford to lose their good political standing, and so they took it upon themselves to deal with this political threat "internally" by plotting to kill Paul. The real concern of the non-believing Jews in Thessalonica was not Paul's theological view about the kingship of Jesus. Their main concern was being identified with the believing Jews and how this would affect their political standing before the Romans.

The Bereans expressed no concern for their social or political standing. Even in the area of doctrinal beliefs, they showed that their main goal was the pursuit of truth rather than an opportunity to advance their own interpretation of Scripture. This explains their openness to listen to Paul's message. Luke described their eagerness as noble, a characterization he did not use for the Thessalonians or the Athenians. In the case of the latter, their eagerness to listen to Paul was evidence of their willingness to accept any novel ideas, rather than their noble character.

In sum, Paul encountered groups of people who, based on societal expectations, possessed something that placed them in some position of power. Some had wealth, some had theological acumen, and some had political influence. As long as those who possessed these were not compelled to use them to assert or hold on to power, hospitality was practised. Otherwise, there was hostility.

6

Housed in a Prison, Imprisoned in a House, Still Unhomed

As we journeyed with Paul from Tarsus to Jerusalem, from Antioch of Syria to the regions of Galatia, Macedonia, Achaia, and Asia, we witnessed through Luke's accounts the repeated back-and-forth transitions of Paul – from enjoying hospitality and being at-home to suffering hostility and being unhomed. There is no denying that religious and theological differences, racial and ethnic tensions, language barriers, social and economic status, and political standing each contributed to the friendship or animosity between the missionary and his audiences. However, on several occasions, the one factor that determined whether Paul was received with hospitality or rejected with hostility was the extent to which Paul or his message posed a threat to the power of his audience. This power came from these people's influence over others or their social standing. Did this trend continue in the remaining portions of the book of Acts? We discuss this question in this chapter.

Unhomed in Ephesus, At-Home with Tyrian and Caesarean Believers, At-Home with the Believers in Jerusalem

From Ephesus, Paul sailed to the port city of Tyre, and from there he sailed again to Caesarea before travelling by land to Jerusalem (Acts 21:3, 7). There were believers in Tyre who hosted Paul for a week,[1] and provided him a temporary home. The same community of believers also warned Paul "through the Spirit" about going to Jerusalem (21:4). Given the mixed composition of

---

1. Given the distance between Jerusalem and Tyre, it is possible that this congregation was started by some Greek speaking Christians from Jerusalem who were dispersed after Stephen's death (Bruce, *The Book of Acts*, 399).

the congregation at Caesarea, their hospitality toward Paul was to be expected. What is noteworthy is that Philip, the evangelist, was the one who provided a temporary home for Paul for another week (21:8). It is important to note that while Philip was Paul's brother in the Lord, the evangelist was also the missionary's former nemesis.[2] This means that the hospitality Philip offered was more than just compliance with a cultural expectation; it was an expression of love and forgiveness to a *repentant* and *transformed* murderer, which are the two most important yet least emphasized elements in our often-romanticized idea of forgiveness.

The Spirit's work is once again seen through the prophetic utterances of Philip's daughter and Agabus, who both spoke about Paul's arrest (21:11). The warning from Agabus about the apostle's arrest was possibly the same message given through the believers at Tyre. Unlike the Spirit's work in Acts 16:6–7, here the Spirit simply revealed what was about to happen to Paul; it was not a prohibition for Paul to go to Jerusalem. This explains why Paul insisted on going (21:12–13). So, while the believers "returned home" (21:6) bidding farewell to Paul, he left these temporary homes and prepared to move to Jerusalem, which typically required a four-day journey.[3]

Paul's visit to Jerusalem on this occasion was his sixth recorded visit in Acts. Luke detailed the transformation of Paul from being a persecutor of the believers on his first visit (8:1), to a new believer trying to find a home but being rejected until Barnabas defended him on his second visit (9:26–31), to becoming an apprentice of Barnabas who brought relief from Antioch to the famine-stricken believers on his third visit (11:27–30; 12:25), to becoming a visiting Antiochene missionary on his fourth visit (13:13), and to becoming a Christian theologian and missionary representing the Syrian church in the discussion on the circumcision of the Gentiles on his fifth visit (15:2). Once again, Paul was visiting as a Christian who remained devoted to his Jewish faith and as a worshipper of God who simply wanted to visit and celebrate the Pentecost or Feast of Weeks with other Jewish devotees (20:16), perhaps not knowing this would be his last visit before being arrested and imprisoned eventually took him to Rome.

Throughout the periods Paul frequented Jerusalem, "home" also changed significantly. As a Jew, Judea was home as his place of origin, yet not quite

---

2. For sure, these former enemies had too many stories to tell. A report that the two former enemies were staying together would have brought a lot of people to meet them, which provided Luke with a perfect venue to gather materials for his work (Keener, *Acts*, 3:3089).

3. Schnabel, *Acts*, 859.

home as a resident of Tarsus. As a student of the law, he could be at-home because he was being taught sociocultural and religious values to which he was accustomed; however, as someone from the diaspora, there was a degree of foreignness in him in relation to the local Jews. As a zealous Jew who expressed his zeal by persecuting the Christians in Jerusalem, he was definitely at-home with the religious authorities and, as Luke underscored, an unwelcome visitor among the Christians (9:26–31). After Barnabas vouched for him, he found a new home in Jerusalem among the Christians, which made him an enemy of the zealous and unbelieving Jews, a group with which he had formerly been at-home, but from whom he had since become unhomed.

This enmity that Paul experienced among the zealous but unbelieving Jews was partly brought about by the false report circulating about him. Even among the believers, there were those who shared the same zeal for the law so, for their sake, James advised Paul to ensure he continued observing the regulations. As James explained to Paul

> You see, brother, how many thousands there are among the Jews of those who have believed. They are all zealous for the law, and they have been told about you that you teach all the Jews who are among the Gentiles to forsake Moses, telling them not to circumcise their children or walk according to our customs. (21:20–21)

There is power in misinformation. Long before there was social media, false reports were already being spread within the networks of Jewish diaspora. Paul was clearly slandered, and a bad reputation had gone before him in many places. So, James advised him to make his observance of the law visible among the Jews (21:23–24).

The laws concerning the Nazirites are clearly expressed in Numbers 6:1–21. Paul might have just completed his vows when he got his haircut at Cenchreae (Acts 18:18), albeit informally, because he could not have fulfilled all the requirements of the vow outside Jerusalem, for example, burning his hair at the tent of meeting (Num 6:18). There were brothers in Jerusalem who made the same vow upon Paul's arrival in Jerusalem. Clues from Josephus suggest that one could associate with others who were making the vow by shouldering the cost of their offering, similar to what Herod Agrippa I did, which was considered an act of piety (*Jewish Antiquities* 19.6.1 §294).[4] Defraying the cost of the men's offerings could reflect Paul's piety and dedication to

---

4. Bruce, *The Book of Acts*, 405 n. 34.

the law, but this was not enough to convince the Jews that their accusations against him were false.

Unhomed Among the Ephesian Jews in Jerusalem, the Roman Tribunal and Jewish Council, "Housed" in Caesarean Prison

"If it were a matter of wrongdoing or vicious crime, O Jews, I would have reason to accept your complaint. But since it is a matter of questions about words and names and your own law, see to it yourselves. I refuse to be a judge of these things" (Acts 18:14–15). These are the words of Gallio when the unbelieving Jewish Corinthians accused Paul of persuading people to worship God contrary to the law (18:13). On the one hand, Gallio can be commended for distinguishing between intra-religious disputes and real criminal cases that should be tried before him. On the other hand, his passivity and unwillingness to take pre-emptive measures in a situation that could potentially lead to violence against innocent citizens were far from commendable (cf. Philo, *Against Flaccus* 1.6 §§39–40).

In contrast to Gallio, the Roman authorities in Jerusalem were quick to act. When some Jewish Ephesians saw Paul in the temple,[5] and having seen him earlier with Trophimus (a Gentile), they "stirred up the crowd and laid hands on him" (21:27). They accused Paul of (1) teaching among the diasporan Jews against the Jews and the law (21:20–21) and (2) defiling the temple by bringing a Gentile into it (21:28–30). This resulted in mass chaos with some zealous but unbelieving Jews attempting to kill Paul. The situation was resolved only when the Roman soldiers intervened and brought Paul to the Roman tribune (21:31–32). The Jewish Ephesians' accusations had to do with the law, as was in the case at Corinth. On the surface, it was a matter that should have been settled internally but the impending violence was so serious that Roman intervention was deemed necessary, especially since Paul's life was in danger. On the one hand, the Roman authorities in Jerusalem should be commended because, unlike Gallio, they were not passive. On the other hand, by arresting Paul and not those who instigated the violence, the snowball of injustice against the apostle began rolling downhill. This was by no means commendable.

---

5. The dispersion had been part of the Jewish identity. This was not the portion of their history that was pleasant to remember, and so many Jews desired to return (Gruen, *Diaspora*, 232). Paul's constant visit to Jerusalem could be an expression of this desire to be home.

Even before Paul arrived in Jerusalem, the false report had been circulating among the Jews.[6] As earlier noted, for this reason, James advised Paul upon his arrival to take four men with him through the process of purification so that there would be evidence that the accusations against him were untrue (21:23–24). As the story unfolded, Paul's observance of the law was not enough to change the minds of the zealous Jews about him. As a result, he remained unwelcome and unhomed, was brought to trial before the Roman tribunal (21:27–22:29) and the Jewish council (22:30–23:11), and was eventually housed in a prison in Caesarea (23:23–26:32).

Unhomed Among the Romans, Unhomed Among the Unbelieving Jews in Jerusalem, Housed in a Prison

Paul's earlier zeal and commitment to the law had motivated him to persecute the disciples in Jerusalem (Phil 3:6; Acts 9:1–2). The tables had turned, and now Paul was on the receiving end of persecution.[7] The zeal by the unbelieving Jews from Ephesus would become more evident later when they vowed not to eat or drink until they had killed Paul (23:12). Credit must be given to the Roman tribune for intervening – it prevented the crowd from causing Paul more harm (21:31–36) – and for allowing Paul to defend himself (21:37–22:21). However, the question remains as to why the instigators of the riot were not arrested or even called in for interrogation, especially as it was the Jewish Ephesians that started the riot and not Paul.

Luke established earlier that the twofold accusation against Paul was false (21:20–21), and the right thing for the Romans to do was to set him free. However, placing Paul in Roman custody is understandable considering the number of witnesses who brought accusations against him. Moreover, being in Roman custody worked to Paul's advantage temporarily because it provided Paul with protection from the hostility and impulsivity of zealous devotees and a gullible crowd. Being under Roman custody, while having some advantages,

---

6. Keener notes that the false reports about Paul would have inevitably raised suspicions about the believers who supported him as being "soft" toward outsiders, thus appearing to be traitors (*Acts*, 3:3131). In this way, they, too, were in danger of being unhomed in their own hometown.

7. A key piece of information was their accusation that Paul brought Trophimus into the temple. Bruce explains that the Romans were quite sympathetic to the Jewish law restricting Gentiles from entering certain sections of the temple. Titus reminded the Jews who were defending the temple (see Josephus, *Jewish Wars* 6.2.4 §126) that they were willing to execute trespassers even if they were Roman citizens (*The Book of Acts*, 407, n. 47).

was far from ideal. It protected Paul from the hostile crowd,[8] but not from the brutality of the Roman authorities. This was when Paul brought up his Roman citizenship (22:25).[9]

In sum, Paul *the believing Jew* was unhomed among the unbelieving Jews (including both the locals and those from diaspora) on account of their zeal for the law and his devotion to Christ. In addition, Paul the *Roman citizen* was unhomed among the Romans, whose exercise of authority raises serious questions, and Paul the *Christian* was "unhomed" among his fellow believers because they, too, were in a delicate situation and could not provide the protection Paul needed at this time. Paul was a Jew unhomed among unbelieving Jews, a Roman unhomed among indifferent Romans, and a Christian unhomed among powerless Christians.

The story took an unexpected turn when Paul was brought to trial before the Sanhedrin, which was composed of Sadducees and members of the Pharisaic movement. In his defense against the accusations that he taught the diasporan Jews not to follow the law (21:20–21), Paul had earlier clarified before the angry crowd

> I am a Jew, born in Tarsus in Cilicia, but brought up in this city, educated at the feet of Gamaliel according to the strict manner of the law of our fathers, being zealous for God as all of you are this day. I persecuted this Way to the death, binding and delivering to prison both men and women, *as the high priest and the whole council of elders can bear me witness*. From them I received letters to the brothers, and I journeyed toward Damascus to take those also who were there and bring them in bonds to Jerusalem to be punished. (22:3–5, italics mine)

Speaking to the Jews in Hebrew might have resulted in their silence (22:2), but it was a temporary silence and did not quell their anger against Paul. Paul's testimony was not enough to convince the crowd of his commitment to the law, however his trial before the Sanhedrin could have taken a different turn had "the high priest and the whole council of elders" testified that his claims were true. When Ananias the high priest slapped Paul's face during the trial (23:2–5), it became clear that the religious authorities with whom Paul had allied himself earlier and expected to come to his protection were now unwilling to come to

---

8. The purpose of Roman custody was both punitive and protective, as Rapske underscores (see his *Paul in Roman Custody*, 10).

9. The Romans were not inclined to favor Paul's Jewish accusers, but they succeeded in getting Paul arrested, thus keeping him from continuing in his work (Keener, *Acts*, 3:3146).

his aid. The action of Ananias was improper, even illegal,[10] because it presumed guilt even before the start of the trial. Ananias got away with his unlawful act because the bystanders were quick to defend the high priest (23:4).

Luke recounted that Paul, after seeing there were Pharisees in the council, appealed to their shared belief in the resurrection (23:6). Thus he found some defenders within the council, but this was not enough to set him free (23:7–10).[11] More importantly, it was not enough to prevent the unbelieving Jews from plotting to once and for all end their dilemma by having Paul killed (23:12–22); however, the plot was discovered by Paul's nephew which saved Paul's life. (This was the plot made with a vow not to eat or drink until they killed Paul.) Paul was able to escape, but that does not mean that the plotters eventually died either of starvation or dehydration, as there were provisions within the Jewish traditions to nullify vows (e.g., Mishnah, Shevu'ot 3:1; Jerusalem Talmud, Sukkah 5:2 §1).[12] That these plotters were willing to pronounce a curse (Greek, *anathematizō*) upon themselves showed the extent of their hatred for Paul. For the plotters, there was no place in their city or anywhere in this world for Paul to consider home – the only place where there would be space for Paul to call home would be the land of the dead.

Paul's testimony was not enough to abate the Jewish crowd's fury; his status and citizenship were not enough to spare him from the Romans' brutality; his earlier zeal was not enough to rally the Jewish authorities to protect him; and, while his theological affiliation with the Pharisees was enough to gain their sympathy, their unified voice was not sufficient to convince the council to free him. The Pharisees were muted and the Christians in Jerusalem were totally out of the picture. With the threat to his life, it was clear that there was no longer any safe place for Paul in Jerusalem. Unhomed in Jerusalem, he was taken to Caesarea and placed in a prison (23:23).

Unhomed in Jerusalem, Housed in a Prison in Caesarea

Paul's trial before the Sanhedrin was so tense that he was almost physically ripped to pieces. As Luke described it, "when the dissension became violent, the tribune, afraid that Paul would be torn to pieces by them, commanded the

---

10. Bruce, *The Book of Acts*, 427.

11. The Pharisees were a minority in the Sanhedrin (Bruce, *The Book of Acts*, 428). This means their presence was not enough to steer the body in Paul's favor. Nonetheless, it was enough to show the invalidity of the accusations against him.

12. Keener, *Acts*, 3:3304.

soldiers to go down and take him away from among them by force and bring him into the barracks" (Acts 23:10). The issue discussed was so controversial that the honorable Sanhedrin could not even follow proper decorum.[13] Following this trial, God revealed to the apostle that he would eventually go to Rome to be a witness (23:11). This did not happen immediately because Paul first spent a couple of years as a prisoner in Caesarea.

Paul was housed in prison in Caesarea for a crime that even the commander of the Roman army in Jerusalem, Claudius Lysias, did not know. Thus Claudius Lysias wrote succinctly to Governor Felix and made clear a few things: (1) the Jews had seized Paul and wanted to kill him for reasons that were unclear at that time (23:27–28); (2) Paul was a Roman citizen (23:27) (however he did not disclose that the Roman soldiers had beaten him, 22:23–25); (3) Claudius had brought Paul before the Jewish council and discovered that the charges had to do with the Jewish law (23:29) (he also did not mention that the Jews had beaten Paul during this trial); (4) Paul did nothing that deserved death or imprisonment (23:29); and (5) there was a plot to kill Paul so Claudius sent Paul to Felix in order that the accusers could bring their charges before him (23:30).

Setting Paul free was not ideal because there was a zealous mob waiting for opportunities to kill him, thus putting his life in danger. Placing him under Roman custody seemed to be a safer option for him because the guards could protect him from the angry crowd. While doing so gave the Romans a chance to further investigate the real reasons for the uproar, keeping him was unjust considering the result of the initial trials which Claudius summed up with the words, "I found that he was being accused about questions of their law, but charged with nothing deserving death or imprisonment" (23:29).

The Jewish authorities were represented by a prosecutor identified as Tertullus, who referred to Paul as a "plague," an instigator of riots, and a ringleader of what was considered an insurrectionist group (24:2). The derisive description implied that Paul was the cause of the deterioration of society, a "civic affliction" that caused political unrest.[14] Name-calling is a way to say, "He is not one of us." Adding to his derogatory remarks were two false accusations that stripped Paul of his rights to live among the free and made the prison his home.

Paul remained in his Caesarean prison for more than two years. Several factors contributed to this tragedy. First, some Jewish religious authorities in Jerusalem and their zealous followers were determined to put Paul to death.

---

13. Keener, *Acts*, 3:3295.
14. Keener, *Acts*, 4:3374.

The false report that circulated prior to Paul's arrival included only one thing – that Paul taught the diasporan Jews to forsake Moses by not practicing the custom of circumcision (21:21). When Paul's case was initially heard by the Roman tribune in Jerusalem, another element was added – that he also defiled the temple by bringing in a Gentile (21:28–29). When the representatives of the high priest brought charges against Paul for the first time before the Roman procurator Felix in Caesarea, yet more charges were levelled against him, "For we have found this man a plague, one who stirs up riots among all the Jews throughout the world and is a ringleader of the sect of the Nazarenes. He even tried to profane the temple, but we seized him" (24:5–6). This so-called riot was more than just a disorderly conduct of a mass of people for the Greek *stasis* carries the idea of insurrection.[15]

It was clear in Luke's earlier account that the Jews from Ephesus started the riot (21:27), but now the story was reversed. A more serious charge of insurrection was brought against him, clearly to make sure that the Romans could no longer argue that Paul's "crime" had only to do with matters of the Jewish religion.

The fact that they have to keep changing the charges they brought against Paul show that the Jewish authorities were relentless in finding reasons to put him away. All these began with a doctrinal dispute between zealous Jews who insisted on circumcising the Gentiles (15:1), and the apostles in Jerusalem making a decision favorable to Paul's stance (15:22–35). False reports about Paul spread in *many* (not all) Jewish diaspora communities (21:21; see also 28:21–24), that James had to advise Paul to perform a nazirite vow as a proof that he was not abandoning his Jewish faith (21:22–24). Aside from some Pharisees who opposed Paul's view that Gentiles do not need to be circumcised (15:5), there were also priests that opposed Paul with no clear charges (23:2–4), but Paul got the support of the Pharisees within the Sanhedrin on account of their shared belief in the resurrection (23:6–10). When the representatives of the priests brought charges to governor Felix in Caesarea, they added the charge of subversion against Paul (24:5).

The matter was not settled during the time of Felix, so the representatives of the high priest had to present their case against Paul to Felix's successor, Festus, but this time with a request to bring Paul to Jerusalem for trial so that they could ambush Paul on the way (25:2–3). The charge of rebellion is so serious that even Jewish authorities do not have the right to request for Paul's release so they can conduct their own trial in Jerusalem. For the representative

---

15. BDAG, s.v. *stasis*.

of the priests to make such a request before Festus, the successor of Felix, is a clear proof that their earlier accusation was unsubstantial. Luke also made clear that they were just planning to assassinate Paul (25:2–3), and Festus knew that the charges are weightless (25:18).

Second, the two Roman procurators in Judea who tried Paul's case were both committed to pleasing the Jewish authorities (24:27; 25:9), perhaps to safeguard their political careers in Judea. Setting Paul free is political suicide for Festus, so he had to please the Jews by keeping Paul in custody (25:9), and as a pretext for not setting Paul free despite being convinced of Paul's innocence, Festus made the excuse that because Paul appealed to Caesar, he had to send Paul to Rome (25:8–12, 21; 26:32). On the part of Paul, being held in custody under the Romans protected him from the angry Jews. On the part of Festus, his decision to keep Paul in custody is at best self-serving, and not in the best interest of Paul. There could have been other ways to protect Paul. So, while they both agreed that Paul was innocent, with Felix allowing Paul some freedom to receive visitors while in prison (24:23) and Festus explicitly stating Paul's innocence (25:18), they both chose to keep Paul in prison. Felix was familiar with the Christians' beliefs because his wife was a Jew (24:22); he also understood Paul's message about future judgment (24:25), but his desire to receive a bribe from Paul kept him from doing the right thing (24:26). Moreover, while Festus could not find anything to charge against Paul,[16] he found it expedient to keep the Jewish authorities happy (25:9) so gave the responsibility for making decisions to the tetrarch of Judea, Herod Agrippa II (25:13–17). Festus's indecision led Paul, who had already been imprisoned for more than two years for made-up charges, to appeal to a higher court (25:12).

Third, Agrippa II also refused to decide in favor of Paul, perhaps to avoid political suicide under the guise of deference to the emperor (26:32). As noted above, the charges against Paul kept changing in each trial and eventually led to a petition to execute him without legitimate charges (see Chart 1).

Paul's defenses before Felix, Festus, and Agrippa focused on his devotion to the law – which had led him to the point of persecuting Christians – his calling, his views about the resurrection, and the facts that he had never instigated chaos anywhere and he had never called for rebellion against the emperor. In the course of these trials, there was one decision upon which the Christians

---

16. Festus did not know of Paul's innocence, but there was insufficient evidence against him. If he had declared Paul's innocence, he would have been forced to acquit him (Keener, *Acts*, 4:3460).

in Jerusalem and all Roman authorities agreed – Paul had done nothing that was punishable by death.

> James: "Thus all will know that there is nothing in what they have been told about you, but that you yourself also live in observance of the law." (21:24)
>
> The Pharisees: "We find nothing wrong in this man." (23:9)
>
> Claudius Lysias: "I found that he was being accused about questions of their law, but charged with nothing deserving death or imprisonment." (23:29)

Felix put off Paul's accusers (24:22), ordered that Paul be granted some freedom (24:23), and called Paul so he could hear him preach (24:24), but kept Paul in prison in hope of receiving a bribe (24:26). In short, Felix was unwilling to set Paul free out of greed, not because he found Paul deserving of imprisonment. Luke's account about Felix indirectly suggests that he also found Paul innocent. As for Festus and Agrippa II, they openly declared Paul's innocence.

> Festus: "When the accusers stood up, they brought no charge in his case of such evils as I supposed." (25:18)
>
> Agrippa II and Festus: "This man is doing nothing to deserve death or imprisonment." (26:31)
>
> Paul: "When they had examined me, they wished to set me at liberty, because there was no reason for the death penalty in my case." (28:18)

The question remains as to why Paul was kept in prison. The Roman soldiers who committed brutal acts were not charged (22:23–29). The Jewish Ephesians who started the riot had gone home and were not charged with any crime (21:27–32); also, they did not present their charges against Paul during the trial before Festus and Agrippa II (24:18–19). The Jewish religious authorities were not prosecuted for pressing false charges. Additionally, with Paul in Caesarea, the unbelievers in Jerusalem and the Pharisees in the Jewish council had faded into the background, and there was no one to defend Paul at this time.

This unhomed missionary was waiting only for the Roman authorities of the region to act justly. These events had created a perfect storm for Paul who had no choice other than appeal to the highest authority in the empire. Another storm was waiting for him on his way – a literal one – but his appeal, in addition to seeking justice, also created an opportunity for him to preach the gospel in Rome – something he had been longing for (19:21; cf. 23:11; Rom 1:15).

Chart 1: The Charges Against Paul and His Defenses

The Accusers	The Charges	Paul's Defences
Zealous Jews	Paul was teaching the Jews in diaspora not to circumcise their children and to forsake the law (21:20–21)	He performed purification rites according to the law (as recommended by James) (21:22–24)
Jewish Asians (Ephesians)	Paul taught everyone everywhere against the people, the law, and the temple (21:28)	As a Jew from Tarsus, but who had studied under Gamaliel, he zealously followed the law (22:3) He had persecuted Christians with the approval of the high priest and the council (22:4–5)
	He defiled the temple by bringing a Gentile into it (21:28)	He was sent *to* Gentiles (22:21); he did not bring Gentiles into the temple
Roman tribune before the Jewish council	Nature of Paul's crime unspecified, only clamor to put him away (22:22)	He was a Pharisee who hoped for the resurrection of the dead (23:6)
Ananias, the high priest, and Tertullus, the lawyer, before the governor, Felix	Paul was a plague who stirred up riots among Jews throughout the world and was a ringleader of the sect of the Nazarenes (24:5)	He never stirred up crowds, not in the temple nor any synagogue – he was just there to worship (24:10–12)
	He attempted to profane the temple but was deterred (24:6)	He was in the temple to bring alms and perform purification (24:17–18)
		He believed in the resurrection (24:15)
		Jews from Asia should bring the accusation, but they were not present (24:18–21)

Chief priest and principal men among the Jews before Festus	Numerous charges that they cannot prove (25:7)	He did not commit offences against the Jews and the temple (25:8)
		He did not commit offences against Caesar (25:8)
		If he was guilty, he would not escape death. If he was not, he should not be handed over to the Jews. He appealed to Caesar instead (25:10–11)
Festus before Agrippa	The ruling Jews petitioned to execute Paul, but pressed no charges (25:18)	
	Disputes about religion, Jesus, resurrection (25:19)	He followed religion strictly and had persecuted Christians. He was being tried because of his belief in the resurrection (26:4–11)

Nowhere near Home

Paul waited more than two years to receive a favorable verdict, but to no avail. The Roman authorities could have decided to release Paul quickly, considering that they had not been convinced that Paul's alleged crime was sufficient to convict or detain him, let alone execute him. However, there were zealous Jews and influential Jewish authorities they wanted to please. Felix waited for a bribe (24:26) and Festus was willing to give the zealous Jews the opportunity to stealthily assassinate Paul (25:2–3, 9). With seemingly no recourse left, Paul, as a Roman citizen, appealed to Caesar (25:12). This appeal became a legal technicality that was used later as an excuse by the Jewish governor Herod Agrippa II to avoid responsibility for making the right (but politically sabotaging) decision of setting Paul free (26:32). So, it was eventually decided that Paul be sent to Rome. Paul had to deal with both the Romans and the Jewish authorities. Keener explains, "Paul's concern is not Roman but Jewish jurisdiction; Paul could demand his right as a citizen to be judged without interference from local laws. Paul may refuse the implicit jurisdiction of an incompetent tribunal, the Sanhedrin (even though the final judge was Festus himself (25:9)."[17] The Romans could have simply declared him innocent, but they were torn between pleasing the Jews and doing the right thing. They chose the first option, so Paul was off to Rome.

A centurion of the Augustan Cohort, Julius, was assigned to transport a ship of prisoners to Rome, one of which was Paul. The ship carried two hundred seventy-six passengers (27:37). With a hundred soldiers under Julius's command and perhaps an additional twenty or thirty crew members, it is likely that half of the passengers were prisoners: it seems that some of these had companions with them – certainly Luke, the author of Acts and a coworker of Paul, accompanied Paul.[18] So Paul was not alone in this journey, however, while having a companion definitely provided some comfort for him, it could not reverse Paul's predicament at this point.

Among the Christians scattered throughout the Mediterranean region Paul was a beloved and respected leader. On the ship, he was just a prisoner waiting for his trial. While in the eyes of the soldiers his life, as one of the prisoners, was not that valuable (27:30), Julius, the centurion, treated Paul kindly, allowed him some freedom (27:3), and protected him from harm (27:43), which was a normal way for one Roman citizen to treat another.[19] The centurion's rejection of Paul's suggestion not to embark because of the threat of bad weather was understandable, partly because of his status and because the pilot and owner of the ship had decided to push through (27:11).

The events that happened two years prior to this voyage can be considered a perfect storm that led to Paul's imprisonment in Rome: the rumors that circulated prior to his arrival in Jerusalem, the Jews seeing Paul with a Gentile, the riot caused by the Ephesian Jews, the hostile crowd, the Jewish religious leaders and their false accusations, the Roman procurators who refused to set Paul free despite being convinced of his innocence, and the Jewish governor who settled for technicalities to avoid deciding on Paul's case. On his way to Rome, the unhomed missionary found himself in a storm that resulted in a shipwreck that left all the passengers and crew stranded on the island of Malta. The residents of the island, as Luke recounted, showed them "unusual kindness," even kindling a fire as a sign of their warm welcome (28:1–2). The warmth was replaced by suspicion, particularly against Paul, when a viper

---

17. Keener, *Acts*, 4:3467.

18. Acts 27 is included in the so-called "we-section" in Acts. Luke was with Paul in this journey, perhaps as a companion or he himself was also a prisoner for reasons unspecified in the narrative.

19. Witherington, *Acts*, 760.

clung to him while he was warming himself near the fire (28:3). The natives initially interpreted this incident as a form of divine justice, only to change their minds when Paul suffered no harm – and even began thinking he was a god (28:4–6). The hospitality continued when Publius, the chief of the island, welcomed and entertained them for three days (28:7). His hospitality opened the opportunity for Paul to minister to his sick father and the others on the island who were sick (28:7–10).

The ship took "many days" to sail from Sidon to Cnidus (27:3, 7). When they encountered the storm, they waited another three days before throwing some items off the ship (27:20), and another two weeks on the island of Clauda (27:16, 33), before reaching Malta and were being welcomed by Publius for three days (28:7) spending another three months in Malta before heading to Syracuse (28:11) where they spent three days (28:12), another two days sailing before arriving at Puteoli (28:13), and another week sailing before arriving in Rome (28:14). Having already spent more than two years in the prison in Caesarea, this meant that from the time Paul was arrested in Jerusalem to the time he arrived in Rome, at least two-and-a-half years had gone by. Paul then spent another two years under house arrest in Rome (28:30).

Imprisoned in a Rented House in Rome

Being a citizen of a country is one thing, considering a country as one's home is another. Paul identified Rome as his "country" of citizenship, yet Rome was not home for him. His original plan was to visit the imperial capital as a missionary, but he went there as a prisoner.

At Caesarea, Paul was housed in a prison; at Rome, his house was his prison. In modern times, the needs of prisoners are typically provided for by the state, but this was not so in ancient times.[20] While in Caesarea, Paul's friends had been providing for his needs in prison (24:23); in Rome he had to rent at his own expense a place where he was imprisoned (28:30).[21] If his letter to the Philippians was written within these two years of Roman imprisonment, it is possible that the Christians at Philippi continued supporting Paul (and Luke) during this time (see Phil 1:5–17; 4:10–20). Paul was given some freedom to receive visitors and he was able to preach the word to them (Acts 28:22–23,

---

20. Ramsay, *Paul the Traveller*, 310–13.

21. The standard of living in Rome was high and renting an apartment that would have allowed Paul to welcome visitors and hold meetings suggests that he was able to rent a place that had significant space (Rapske, *Paul in Roman Custody*, 228–39).

30–31). Ironically, some of the Jews in Rome who came to him (presumably voluntarily) also rejected his message (28:24–28),[22] and so his house became a meeting place for people, both Jews and Gentiles, to hear the word.

Paul could have been freed earlier. He claimed innocence before the Jews in Rome (28:18). This is something that has been established repeatedly in Acts by the testimonies of the Roman authorities. The fact that he spent another two years in Rome waiting for his case to be heard suggests that his case was not given priority (28:30) and recalls the period he spent waiting for Felix to make a decision (24:27). Paul's experience of being unhomed continued while he was in Rome. He was no stranger to the Roman believers. While at Corinth, Paul stayed and worked with a diasporan Jewish couple, Priscilla and Aquila, who were from Rome (18:2).[23] It is possible that they had introduced Paul to the other Roman Christians, which explains why Paul had corresponded with them prior to his visit (Rom 1:8–15).[24] His personal greetings in his letter to them show that he had known a number of members within the community (16:1–16). He had been planning to visit them on his way to Illyricum (15:18–19) and Spain (15:22–23). However, there had been reports about him among the Roman Christians that Paul had been preaching licentiousness to attract God's grace – which he refuted in his letter (3:8).

Paul originally planned to visit them as an itinerant missionary, but he arrived as a prisoner who came with an appeal to Caesar. Nonetheless, this opened an opportunity for him to minister to the Roman believers, although some of the Jews rejected his message. Despite his innocence, he remained under Roman custody. However, the sufferings Paul endured for four-and-a-half years concluded with an opportunity for him to preach the good news in Rome. Through his imprisonment remarkable opportunities opened; both the Jews and Gentiles in Rome benefitted from Paul's experience of being unhomed.

---

22. By the time Paul arrived at Rome, the Jews had been living in Rome for a few centuries already. Aside from politically driven attacks, they had been subjects of some satires that include comments about their religious practices, physical features, and even their diet. See Gruen, *Diaspora*, 15–53.

23. The hospitality of Priscilla and Aquila made them the perfect example of what Paul instructed the Romans to do – be hospitable. See Andrew B. Spurgeon, *Romans: A Pastoral and Contextual Commentary*, Asia Bible Commentary Series (Carlisle: Langham Global Library, 2020), 211.

24. The Christian congregation in Rome was not the only one Paul had not previously visited but with whom he corresponded. The congregations at Colossae and Laodicea were two similar groups (Col 2:1–5): while the letter to the Colossians survived and was included in the collection of Paul's letters, the letter to the Laodiceans did not (4:16).

Israel Unhomed, Gentiles At-Home

As noted, prior to his arrival at Rome, Paul had already corresponded with the Roman Christians and expressed his desire to visit them (Rom 1:11–13). Two of Paul's coworkers were from Rome, Priscilla and Aquila (Acts 18:2), and it is likely that it was through them that he got acquainted with other members of the Roman congregation. It is possible that the question regarding Israel's place in God's plan for saving the Gentiles was one of the topics he discussed with Roman believers prior to his arrival in Rome. If this is the case, it would explain Luke's concise description of Paul's exposition of Scripture during his two-year ministry at Rome: (1) the kingdom of God and the role of Jesus as the Christ (28:23); (2) the refusal of some Jews in Rome to believe (28:24–26); and (3) the same salvation being offered to the Gentiles (28:28). These issues, especially the last two, were the same ones Paul raised in his letter before he visited them.

Paul elaborated how Israel's rejection of God opened the door for Gentiles to become part of "God's people" (Rom 9–11). It was part of Israel's original calling to be a "kingdom of priests" (Exod 19:6); as priests, they were to function as mediators between God and the rest of humanity. Peter explained their function further by alluding to Isaiah's description of Israel's task of proclaiming God's excellencies to the nations (Isa 43:21; cf. 1 Pet 2:9). Isaiah also reminded Israel that God had made them his covenant people so that they would be a light to the Gentiles (Isa 42:6; cf. 49:6; 60:3). Israel did not fulfil this function: when Jesus came, *he* took that function (Luke 2:32). This was the same function Paul claimed to share with Christ (Acts 13:47), so he made it his mission to reach out to the Gentiles. This task was also given to the disciples when Jesus commissioned them to make disciples of all Gentiles (Greek, *ethnē*; translated as "nations" in English Bibles; see Matt 28:19). In other words, what Israel failed to do, Jesus would fulfil.

Paul explained the reason for Israel's failure in bringing the message of God's kingdom to the rest of the nations in this way: the Israelites themselves did not believe the message (Rom 9:30–33). Their rejection of God resulted in God's rejection of them. It also opened a door for the Gentiles to find home in God and, most importantly, made it abundantly clear that the Gentiles' enjoyment of the covenant is based on God's promise to Abraham to bless all the nations (and is fulfilled through Jesus). Wright explains Israel's rejection this way.

> Thus Israel, as the Messiah's people, is seen to have exercised its vocational instrumentality in God's rescue operation for the world

precisely by acting out that newly discovered and deeply shocking "messianic" vocation: Israel is indeed the means of bringing God's rescue to the world, but it will be through Israel's acting out of the Messiah-shaped vocation, of being "cast away" for the sake of the world. Paul finally says it out loud (at a point where most interpreters have long since lost the thread and so fail to make the connection) in 11.12, 15; this is where we see why Paul did not deny the "boast" of 2.19–20, but went on affirming it paradoxically, even though it raised the questions of 3.1–8 to which he has at last returned and which he has at last answered. Salvation has come to the Gentiles – through Israel's *paraptōma*, the "stumble" in which Israel recapitulates the sin of Adam, as in 5.20. "The reconciliation of the world" has come about – through Israel's *apobolē*, "casting away," the "rejection" in which Israel recapitulates the death of the Messiah, as in 5.10–11. At the heart of one of Paul's strangest and most challenging chapters we find exactly this theme: that the creator God, having entered into a covenant with Abraham's family that he would bless the world through that family, has been faithful to his promise, even though it has been in the upside-down and inside-out way now unveiled in the Messiah.[25]

No wonder Paul warned the Gentiles not to be boastful about being recipients of God's grace (11:22–24). Moreover, Paul reminded the Roman Christians to show hospitality toward those who might differ in conviction on matters of food and observance of holidays (14:1–3). The point is to remember that whether a person is a Jew or a Gentile, observes a certain diet or special days (or not), everyone depends on God – who allows us to be at-home with him.

Homeward Bound

Paul expressed his personal philosophy of life and death, and his ministry as follows.

> So we are always of good courage. We know that while we are at home in the body we are away from the Lord, for we walk by faith, not by sight. Yes, we are of good courage, and we would rather be

---

25. Wright, *Paul and the Faithfulness of God*, 500. See also Alex Kyrychenko, "The Consistency of Romans 9–11," *Restoration Quarterly* 45, no. 4 (2003): 215–27.

away from the body and at home with the Lord. So whether we are at home or away, we make it our aim to please him. (2 Cor 5:6–9)

Succinctly, for Paul, to be at-home in the body was to be away from the Lord, and conversely, to be away from the body was to be at-home in the Lord. The expression did not deny God's presence in his life and ministry. His attempt to please the Lord suggested an acknowledgement of God's presence, and elsewhere in the same letter, he recognized God's empowerment (12:9). Several years after writing to the Corinthians, he once again acknowledged God's presence and strengthening as he faced the numerous threats in ministry (2 Tim 4:17) and expressed the hope that despite the dangers he faced, "The Lord will rescue [him] from every evil deed and bring [him] safely into [God's] heavenly kingdom" (4:18). Paul also hinted in this letter that his death was imminent (4:6); in other words, he would soon be away from the body to be at-home with the Lord.

In the biblical account, Luke concluded the book of Acts with Paul's imprisonment in Rome. There is no other account in Acts about the deaths of the remaining apostles after the death of Judas, except that of James (Acts 12:1–3), so we have to rely on works outside the Bible to shed light on Paul's death. Paul's Roman imprisonment in Acts 28, according to Eusebius, was not his last. Despite being in detention, Paul enjoyed some degree of freedom (28:30–31).[26] According to Eusebius, Paul was able to enjoy such freedom because "Nero was more disposed to mildness in the beginning," and the emperor even received Paul's defense (Eusebius, *Ecclesiastical History* 2.22.8). The historian further explained that Paul's death did not happen during Paul's imprisonment in Rome as recorded in Acts, interpreting Paul's statement about his "first defense" and his deliverance from "the mouth of the lion" (2 Tim 4:16–17) to mean that he was released from prison and was taken under Roman custody again later when Nero deteriorated to become a tyrant (Eusebius, *Ecclesiastical History* 2.22.6–8).[27]

Years prior to his death, Paul had already recounted the multiple times he was imprisoned, his labor, and the other types of sufferings he had endured for the sake of his ministry (2 Cor 11:23–27). Between the writing of 2 Corin-

---

26. Eusebius, *Ecclesiastical History: Complete and Unabridged*, New Updated Edition, trans. C. F. Cruse (Peabody: Hendrickson, 1998).

27. For a fuller discussion on the circumstances surrounding the writing of 2 Timothy and the question of Paul's second Roman imprisonment, see Michael Prior, *Paul the Letter-Writer and the Second Letter to Timothy*, Journal for the Study of New Testament Supplement Series 23 (Sheffield: JSOT Press, 1989), 70–90.

thians and 2 Timothy, there was more that could have been added to the list. This explains why Paul claimed, "I have fought the good fight, I have finished the race, I have kept the faith" (2 Tim 4:7). After dedicating his life to faithful service, he was ready "to be poured out like a drink offering," to "depart,"[28] and to stand before the righteous judge (4:6, 8). These are images he used to refer to his death. As already mentioned earlier, Paul also referred to his death as being home with God (2 Cor 5:6–9).[29] Paul's life was truly exemplary and remarkable. After years of service to the Lord, he was ready to be at-home with the Lord.

Loss of Power and Being Unhomed

The last few years of Paul's ministry leading to his imprisonment were characterized by endurance on the part of the apostle and by abuse of power on the part of those in authority. The Jewish Christians, both those in Judea and those in diaspora, had long welcomed the former persecutor-become-transformed disciple of Christ. Even Philip, whose life was endangered because of the persecution Paul spearheaded against the Christians, did not use his influence to malign and discredit Paul (Acts 21:8), but along with the other believers, he made the apostle at-home in their community. It was the non-believing Jews who went from place to place to spread false stories about Paul (21:21) that maligned and threatened Paul. Their central dispute with Paul's teaching was that Gentiles no longer needed to be circumcised to become members of God's community. Even among the believing Jews, some, like the believing Pharisees, did not consider this a positive development. Two things could potentially have resulted from removing the requirement of circumcision: first, the Jews would have had less control over those who were joining the community, and second, more Gentiles would have been able to join the community. Once again, power was at play.

Paul's trials before Roman proconsuls, Jewish governors, and the Sanhedrin also illustrate how power can be abused and, in the process, promote injustice. Paul asserted his rights as a Roman citizen twice, but these were not enough for him to receive a fair hearing. Luke's accounts show that the Roman officials had no qualms about using their authority to: enrich themselves by receiving bribes,

---

28. The word *analusis* (translated "departure") means departing to return home (e.g. Josephus, *Antiquities* 6.4.1 §52; 19.1.7 §46; 11.3.1 §31), but in the Greek Old Testament, it is a euphemism for death. See Prior, *Paul the Letter-Writer*, 109 n. 59, 210.

29. This expression is comparable to the Greek idea of the soul's "liberation from the body." See Prior, *Paul the Letter-Writer*, 100.

advance their own political careers, protect their self-interests, use brutality to break the powerless into submission. Luke's portrayal of the Jewish religious authorities is no more flattering than his portrayal of the Roman authorities. Although Paul appealed to the incongruent beliefs of the Pharisees and Sadducees regarding the resurrection and found sympathy among his fellow Pharisees, his teaching about the resurrection was not the main reason he was on trial. With the growing influence of Christians on the Jews, the influence of the religious authorities diminished. The Pharisees and the Sadducees had been at odds regarding the issue of the resurrection for many years, yet there seems to be no record of violence resulting from their theological debates. Apparently, for these two religious groups, even the doctrine of the resurrection was not something worth *dying for*. But when the Christians began to gain traction among the Jews, the religious authorities began to see their loss of influence as something worth *killing for*. This explains why Jesus was unjustly sentenced to death, and why Paul had to endure violence and hardship. He was imprisoned in a house, and still unhomed.

7

Unhomed with Human Power, At-Home with Divine Presence

With all the privileges that came with his family of origin and the credentials he personally achieved, Paul could have enjoyed good standing wherever he went. He had impressive credentials on paper, but his encounter with the risen Lord changed the way he looked at his social capital. He came to the realization that whatever "gains" he achieved were essentially "losses" compared to the value of knowing Christ and the power of his resurrection (Phil 3:7–10). Power comes with credentials and status; there is also power in the resurrection of Jesus. Paul acknowledged the importance of both but considered the latter more important because it is the one that has eternal value.

Prior to his encounter with Christ on the road to Damascus, Paul did not only understand the holding of human authorities and powers, he was willing to use them to advance his own agenda. He acted out of religious zeal, but his means to uphold the honor of his beliefs were atrocious. As those following the Way of Jesus gained more influence among the Jews, the Jewish authorities lost more of their power over the people. The zealous yet unbelieving Paul could not take this sitting down, so he spearheaded the campaign against those who later became known as Christians, violently attacking them. The increasing influence of the Christians threatened the power and authority of the Jewish leaders, and they would not allow this to prosper. In response, he was willing to do harm, all in the name of God. Paul did not carry out his actions from a defensive stance. Clearly, for him, his beliefs were worth killing for. Paul persecuted the Christians, causing them to be dislocated, or "unhomed." He acted from a position of power, removing the Christians from their homes to be scattered abroad, but all this would change after his personal encounter with Christ.

Wealth, social and political standing, education, and, to some degree, fluency in a language are factors that place one person above others in a social hierarchy. Some even consider their race, ethnic origin, religious background, and cultural practices to be things that make them superior over others. While some of these things make certain groups more powerful than others in particular societal structures, we have seen in the previous chapters that the social dynamics between various social classes depend primarily on whether those on top of the social hierarchy use the power and authority inherent in their class constructively (e.g. by being a servant to others) or destructively (e.g. by causing others to be unhomed).

This was the pattern in the ministry of Paul. Ethnic and racial tensions were realities the first-century Jews had to deal with. Religion and ethnicity were closely linked together, and so intermarriages were not really considered a positive cultural practice (e.g. Ezra 9:13–15; 10:2, 10, 17–18; Neh 13:27). Moreover, there were certain portions of the temple in Jerusalem where Gentiles were prohibited. Having religious prohibitions is not necessarily a bad thing. The Jews had the right to exercise their religion including requiring Gentiles to be circumcised, and proselytes were happy to comply with those rules. Similarly, Christians had the right not to impose circumcision on Gentiles who believed in Jesus. Before the Christians came to this conclusion, some believing Jews pushed back against this freedom given to the Gentile believers. For Paul, circumcision was one of the ethnic markers of the Jews and, therefore, not to be imposed on Gentiles who professed their faith in Christ. Gentile believers did not need to be unhomed just because they were uncircumcised. Language was also not a barrier to believers in making those of different ethnicities feel at-home. The Lycaonians had shown hospitality to Paul despite language differences (Acts 14:11–13). Paul's ministry to the Gentiles shows that in Christ everyone can be of equal standing before God. Ethnic or language differences were not – and are not – sufficient reason to make others unhomed.

Hospitality is a cultural value commonly practised by people around the Mediterranean during the time of Paul. Many diasporan Jews had extended this courtesy to Paul and his team of missionaries, but this should not be surprising because they shared the same ethnic origin. The Gentile residents of Malta welcomed Paul and the other prisoners who were on board with him when they shipwrecked near the island (28:1–10). Instead of asking the question, "How are you different from me?," those who practised hospitality asked, "How am I similar to you?" Paul extended the same kind of hospitality to the diasporan Jews of Antioch by talking about their shared ancestry and history as he preached the gospel to them (13:13–39). Similarly, he acknowledged his shared humanity with the Athenians when he preached the same gospel to them (17:29). For those who do not have any claim to superiority or any compulsion to make others subservient, language and ethnicity are not reasons to make others unhomed.

The same principle seems to be at work when we discuss theological differences. Gamaliel's advice revealed that the increasing influence of Christians who proclaimed the lordship of Christ and the resurrection of Jesus meant that the Jewish religious authorities were losing their influence. Silencing those who believed in Jesus was not easy. Paul's zeal in doing the "dirty job" of displacing the Christians, even to the point of killing some of them, was welcomed by the religious leaders. Insofar as Paul was willing to maintain the power and influence of the Jewish religious authorities, he enjoyed good standing with them. Submission to religious authorities is right and proper but doing their bidding when it is wrong is displeasing to God.

In Luke's narrative, two things sharply contrasted the traditional Jewish religious authorities and the Christian leaders: the first was their willingness to listen and the second was their use of power. Paul claimed to have received a revelation from the Lord (Gal 1:12) but, even with direct revelation, he was willing to subject himself to the apostles in Jerusalem (2:1–2). Some Christian Pharisees, in contrast, insisted that all Gentiles must adhere to the law in the same way the proselytes did (Acts 15:5). The apostles acted commendably in listening to all points of view before making a decision regarding the matter. Listening is the bare minimum of respectable acts: the apostles' tempered use of power and authority as the leaders of the church and their balancing of adherence to God's standards with flexibility are worth emulating. The apostles did not operate with the principle "follow us or else"; they were clear about the standard to which they should adhere but, beyond that, there could be flexibility. Abusing religious power can easily be presented as "fighting for the truth" or "contending for the faith" (Jude 3). The ruling of the apostles regarding the issue of Gentile adherence to the law shows that, although they were honored as authorities, they acknowledged both their limitations in seeing and interpreting the Scripture in its entirety, and their need to listen to others.

Similarly, the contrast between the Bereans and Thessalonians also included the willingness of the "noble" Bereans to listen and examine the Scripture carefully (Acts 17:11). In contrast to the Bereans, the non-believing Thessalonians responded violently to Paul's message. They claimed that their motivation stemmed from Paul preaching rebellion against Caesar and the idea that there was another king, Jesus (17:7). However, the disturbance the message caused to the leaders of the city suggests their reason was more than just their loyalty to the emperor. The primary reason for their violence against Paul seems to have been political expedience – another reason for Paul becoming unhomed.

Paul's declaration that Jesus is Lord created a strong reaction because, on the surface, it sounded like Paul was instigating an insurgency. However, the messages that Jesus and Paul preached (Matt 22:21; Mark 12:17; Luke 20:25; Rom 13:1) clearly show that they never called their followers to rebel against God-ordained institutions, even as they called people to acknowledge the true king, Christ. It seems the primary concern of the unbelieving Thessalonians was self-preservation. The Romans might not have been able to distinguish the Christian Jews in Thessalonica from the non-believing ones, and if the Romans heard that "the Jews of Thessalonica" were proclaiming that Jesus is king, the Thessalonian Jews might have lost their privileged standing before Rome. So, they opted to use violence to silence Paul and the Christians in order to maintain their power in society.

In addition to the aforementioned reasons, power is also inherent in wealth and the status that accompanies it in the social hierarchy. How one uses this power can make others feel at-home or unhomed. In Acts, we read stories of wealthy people who used their power and influence to show hospitality to others. Lydia and the Macedonians are examples of this. With their wealth, they made Paul feel at-home in the community. Lydia was not even sure if she was worthy to show hospitality to the Lord's workers (Acts 16:15). Their generosity was offered with no strings attached. Their mentality was not "I gave to you and your work; therefore, I have power over you." In contrast, some Corinthians (Christians!) looked at Paul contemptuously. Hints from Paul's letters to the Corinthians suggest that their treatment of Paul communicated this message: "You do not and cannot meet our standards. Our abilities and our social standing make us superior, and we have power over you. We do not even acknowledge your apostleship." This may explain why Paul willingly accepted the Philippians' financial support (Phil 1:5; 4:15) but did not accept support from the Corinthians, even while he was ministering at Corinth (2 Cor 11:9).[1]

As a missionary, Paul experienced being at-home with hospitable communities and being unhomed with hostile communities. There were those who exercised their power for constructive purposes and for building the kingdom of God. There were those who used it for destructive purposes and for

---

1. Luke's version of Jesus's discourse on how the disciples should differ from the Gentile lords and benefactors, "The kings of the Gentiles lord it over them; and those who have authority over them are called 'Benefactors.' But *it is* not this way with you" (Luke 22:25–26 NASB).

strengthening their place in society and religious institutions, even if it meant committing violence against others. The bottom line of all these problems was power – its use and its abuse. Power is like a knife; in the hand of a surgeon, it can save life, but in the hand of a criminal, it can take away life.

As an apostle, Paul was not reluctant to assert his authority – which is evident in his letters to the Corinthians. As a Christian, a man transformed by Christ, he knew the limits of exercising his authority. As a saint, Paul was by no means perfect. In the same way he experienced being unhomed he also caused others to be unhomed, as he had done to Barnabas because of Mark. Luke's account of this conflict was neutral and matter-of-fact; he did not in any way imply that either Paul or Barnabas was right. The pastoral heart of Barnabas was commendable, and Paul's willingness to later change his assessment about John Mark (Col 4:10; 2 Tim 4:11) shows that he was not really one who would excessively assert his authority.

Unhomed in the World, At-Home with the Lord

Paul's ministry shows that hardships are a normal part of serving God. His experience of being in a state of ambivalence, of being at-home yet at the same time unhomed, is familiar to ministers today. We are often dependent on others to make us feel at-home. At times, to put it bluntly, we are at the mercy of those who have some form of power and when they misuse or abuse their power we can feel, and be, unhomed. Power is like perfume. Applying a little of it can make us "smell good" and cause the people around us to feel comfortable, but applying too much of it can cause them breathing difficulties, and ingesting it can poison them and us. Power can be used for something constructive, such as showing hospitality to others, building God's kingdom in the process. With power, we can make others feel at-home. Power can also be used for something destructive, such as showing hostility to others, causing *unnecessary* chaos and dissension within God's community and even in the world. With power, we can cause others to be unhomed.

Power and influence can be used to spread misinformation about others. They can also be used for personal vendettas or advancing personal agendas. The authority that comes with religious hierarchy can be used to silence others, even on issues that are non-essential. Social status that comes with wealth and other credentials, even amid the perceived superiority of other ethnicities and races, can be used unnecessarily to place others in a subservient role. No wonder that in Scripture Jesus taught his disciples about the importance of true humility and servanthood, reminding them that while lording it over others was conventional, "but not so with you" (Luke 22:26). Perhaps a more important question is: if we, as ministers, assume these roles of power, how are we going to exercise our authority?

Paul's experience of being unhomed also taught him valuable lessons about contentment, regardless of one's state in life, and what it means to do all things through Christ who strengthens us (Phil 4:13). His experience also taught him that God's grace is available in one's time of weakness (2 Cor 12:9) and that the Spirit speaks on our behalf in these periods of one's life (Rom 8:26). Moreover, he learned that respect is not a guarantee for those who labor in the Lord (1 Thess 2:9; 5:12) and what it means to "be Christ" in a life with suffering, knowing there is "gain" that awaits (Phil 1:21; cf. Gal 2:20). It is in being unhomed in the world that one can fully experience being at-home in the Lord. It is with this strength that Paul was able to fight a good fight, run the race, and keep the faith (2 Tim 4:7). It is with God's continuous presence that Paul was able to persevere, to look forward to the day that he would no longer be in a state of ambivalence, fully at-home in God's presence, and no longer unhomed.

Bibliography

Adeyemo, Tokunboh. "Religious Pluralism." In *Africa Bible Commentary*, edited by Tokunboh Adeyemo, 1558. Carlisle: HippoBooks, 2006.

Athyal, Jesudas M. "Church and Nationalism." In *South Asia Bible Commentary*, edited by Brian Wintle et al., 1545. Rajasthan: Open Door Publications, 2015.

Augustine. *On Christian Doctrine and Selected Introductory Works*. Edited by Timothy George. Theological Foundations. Nashville: B&H Academic, 2022.

Aune, David E. *Prophecy in Early Christianity and the Ancient Mediterranean World*. Grand Rapids: Eerdmans, 1983.

Barclay, John M. G. "Paul Among Diaspora Jews: Anomaly or Apostate?" *Journal for the Study of the New Testament* 18, no. 60 (1996): 89–120.

Barrett, C. K. *The Acts of the Apostles*. International Critical Commentary, 2 vols. Edinburgh: T&T Clark, 1994.

Bauckham, Richard. *Jesus and the Eyewitnesses: The Gospels as Eyewitness Testimony*. Grand Rapids: Eerdmans, 2006.

Betz, Hans Dieter. *Galatians*. Philadelphia: Fortress Press, 1979.

Bruce, F. F. *Paul: Apostle of the Free Spirit*. Exeter: Paternoster Press, 1977.

_____. *The Book of Acts*. The New International Commentary on the New Testament, rev ed. Grand Rapids: Eerdmans, 1988.

Charlesworth, James H., ed. *The Old Testament Pseudepigrapha*. 2 vols. Garden City: Doubleday, 1983–1985.

Chase, Frederic Henry. *The Credibility of the Books of Acts*. London: Macmillan, 1902.

Chen, Stephen H., Emily Zhang, Cindy H. Liu, and Leslie K. Wang. "Depressive Symptoms in Chinese Immigrant Mothers: Relations with Perceptions of Social Status and Interpersonal Support." *Cultural Diversity & Ethnic Minority Psychology* 27, no. 1 (2021): 72–81.

Chilton, Bruce. *Rabbi Paul: An Intellectual Biography*. New York: Doubleday, 2004.

Danker, Frederick W., Walter Bauer, William F. Arndt, and F. Wilbur Gingrich. *Greek-English Lexicon of the New Testament and Other Early Christian Literature*. 3rd ed. Chicago: University of Chicago Press, 2000.

Deissmann, Adolf. *Paul: A Study in Social and Religious History*, translated by William E. Wilson. New York: Harper & Row, 1957.

De Santa Ana, Julio. "Mission of the Church in a World Torn Between Poor and Rich." *International Review of Mission* 72, no. 1 (1983): 20–31.

DeSilva, David A. *Honor, Patronage, Kinship & Purity: Unlocking New Testament Culture*. Downers Grove: InterVarsity Press, 2000.

Dunn, James D. G. *Beginning from Jerusalem*. Christianity in the Making 2. Grand Rapids: Eerdmans, 2009.

———. *The New Perspective on Paul*, rev ed. Grand Rapids: Eerdmans, 2005.
Elliott, J. K. *The Apocryphal New Testament: A Collection of Apocryphal Christian Literature in an English Translation Based on M. R. James*. New York: Oxford University Press, 1993.
Eusebius. *Ecclesiastical History: Complete and Unabridged*. New Updated Edition. Translated by C. F. Cruse. Peabody: Hendrickson, 1998.
Ferguson, Everett. *Backgrounds of Early Christianity*. Third Edition. Grand Rapids: Eerdmans, 2003.
Foakes-Jackson, F. J., and Kirsopp Lake, *The Beginnings of Christianity*, 5 vols. London: Macmillan, 1933.
Freud, Sigmund. "The 'Uncanny.'" In *The Standard Edition of the Complete Psychological Works of Sigmund Freud*, Vol. 17, translated by Alix Strachey, edited by James Strachey, 218–53. London: Hogwarth Press, 1925.
Frey, Jean-Baptiste. *Corpus Inscriptionum Judaicarum*. 2 vols. Rome: Pontifical Biblical Institute, 1936–1952.
Furusawa, Kentaro. "The Reception of Christianity in Okinawa: On Relations Between the Okinawa Baptist Convention and Native Religion." *Religion and Society* 13, no. 3 (2007): 284–302.
Gabbard, Glen O., and Holly Crisp. *Narcissism and Its Discontents: Diagnostic Dilemmas and Treatment Strategies with Narcissistic Patients*. Washington, DC: American Psychiatric Association Publishing, 2018.
George, Roji Thomas. *Philippians: A Pastoral and Contextual Commentary*. Asia Bible Commentary Series. Cumbria: Langham Global Library, 2019.
Gerhards, Jürgens, and Silke Hans. "From Hasan to Herbert: Name-Giving Patterns of Immigrant Parents between Acculturation and Ethnic Maintenance." *American Journal of Sociology* 114, no. 4 (2009): 1102–28.
Ghazoul, Ferial J. "The Unhomely at Home and Abroad." *Journal of Arabic Literature* 35, no. 1 (2004): 1–24.
Gier, Nicholas F. *The Origins of Religious Violence: An Asian Perspective*. Lanham: Lexington Books, 2014.
Girma, Hewan. "Black Names, Immigrant Names: Navigating Race and Ethnicity Through Personal Names." *Journal of Black Studies* 51, no. 1 (2020): 16–36.
Goh, Daniel P. S., and Terence Chong. "Ministering in the Middle: Christian Megachurches and Minoritarian Politics in Southeast Asia." *Politics and Religion* 15, no. 4 (2022): 722–41.
Golec de Zavala, Agnieszka, Karolina Dyduch-Hazar, and Dorottya Lantos. "Collective Narcissism: Political Consequences of Investing Self-Worth in the Ingroup's Image." *Advances in Political Psychology* 40, supp. 1 (2019): 37–71.
Gruen, Erich S. *Diaspora: Jews Amidst Greeks and Romans*. Cambridge: Harvard University Press, 2002.
Harrán, Dan. "The Jewish Nose in Early Modern Art and Music." *Renaissance Studies* 28, no. 1 (2014): 50–70.

Hawthorne, Gerald F. *Philippians*. Word Biblical Commentary 43. Waco: Word Books, 1983.
Hemer, Colin J. *The Book of Acts in the Setting of Hellenistic History*. Wissenschaftliche Untersuchungen zum Neuen Testament 49. Tübingen: Mohr Siebeck, 1989.
Hengel, Martin. *The Pre-Christian Paul*. London: SCM Press, 1991.
Holloway, Paul A. *Philippians*, edited by Adela Yarbro Collins. Minneapolis: Fortress, 2017.
Josephus. *The Works of Josephus: Complete and Unabridged*. New Updated Version. Translated by William Whiston. Peabody: Hendrickson, 1987.
Kato, Julius-Kei. *How Immigrant Christians Living in Mixed Cultures Interpret Their Religion: Asian-American Diasporic Hybridity and Its Implication for Hermeneutics*. Lewiston: Edwin Mellen Press, 2012.
Keener, Craig S. *Acts: An Exegetical Commentary*. 4 vols. Grand Rapids: Baker Academic, 2012–2015.
Kim, David J. "Four Pillars and Four Diviners: Fate, Fluidity, and Invention in Horoscopic *Saju* Divination in Contemporary South Korea." *Journal of Korean Religions* 10, no. 2 (2019): 301–29.
Kitagawa, Joseph M. "The Asian Mind." *Anglican and Episcopal History* 65, no. 4 (1996): 404–11.
Klausner, Joseph. *From Jesus to Paul*. Translated by William F. Stinespring. New York: Macmillan, 1943.
Kyrychenko, Alex. "The Consistency of Romans 9–11." *Restoration Quarterly* 45, no. 4 (2003): 215–27.
Lee, Chee-Chiew. "Responding to Persecution and Marginalization." In *Exploring the New Testament in Asia: An Evangelical Perspective*, edited by Samson L. Uytanlet and Bennet Lawrence, 209–32. Carlisle: Langham Global Library, 2024.
Levinskaya, Irina A. *The Book of Acts in Its Diaspora Setting*. The Book of Acts in Its First Century Setting 5. Grand Rapids: Eerdmans, 1996.
Liddell, Henry George, Robert Scott, Henry Stuart Jones. *A Greek-English Lexicon*. 9th ed. with revised supplement. Oxford: Clarendon, 1996.
Lührmann, Dieter. *Galatians*. Continental Commentaries, translated by O. C. Dean, Jr. Minneapolis: Fortress Press, 1992.
Malherbe, Abraham J. "A Physical Description of Paul." *Harvard Theological Review* 79, no. 1 (1986): 170–75.
Marshall, Wende Elizabeth. *Potent Mana: Lessons in Power in Healing*. UPCC Book Collections on Project MUSE. Albany: SUNY Press, 2011.
Mendoza, Noli P. "Faith at the Border, Faith on the Move: Migrations, Transitions, and Transformations in Acts 8–11." In *God at the Borders: Globalization, Migration and Diaspora*, edited by Charles R. Ringma, Karen Hollenbeck-Wuest, and Athena O. Gorospe, 253–67. Mandaluyong: OMF Literature, 2005.
Minnen, Peter van. "Paul the Roman Citizen." *Journal for the Study of the New Testament* 17, no. 56 (1995): 43–52.

Mitchell, Margaret M. *John Chrysostom on Paul: Praises and Problem Passages.* Writings from the Greco-Roman World 48. Atlanta: SBL Press, 2022.

Murphy-O'Connor, Jerome. "On the Road and on the Sea with St. Paul." *Bible Research* 1, no. 2 (1985): 38–47.

NiaNia, Wiremu. "Restoring Mana and Taking Care of Wairua: A Story of Māori Whānau Healing." *Australian & New Zealand Journal of Family Therapy* 38, no. 1 (2017): 72–97.

Ortega, Gema. "Where is Home? Diaspora and Hybridity in Contemporary Dialogue." *Moderna Språk* 114, no. 4 (2020): 43–60.

Penner, Todd. *In Praise of Christian Origin: Stephen and the Hellenists in Lukan Apologetic History.* Emory Studies in Early Christianity. New York: T&T Clark, 2004.

Percy, Martyn. "Power and Fundamentalism." *Journal of Contemporary Religion* 10, no. 3 (1995): 273–82.

Philo. *The Complete Works of Philo: Complete and Unabridged.* New Updated Version. Peabody: Hendrickson, 1993.

Prior, Michael. *Paul the Letter-Writer and the Second Letter to Timothy.* Journal for the Study of New Testament Supplement Series 23. Sheffield: JSOT Press, 1989.

Rajak, Tessa. "Synagogue Within the Greco-Roman City." In *Jews, Christians, and Polytheists in the Ancient Synagogue: Cultural Interaction in the Greco-Roman Period,* edited by Stephen Fine, 161–73. London: Routledge, 1999.

Ramsay, William M. *St. Paul the Traveller and Roman Citizen.* New York: Putnam's Sons, 1898.

Rapske, Brian. *Paul in Roman Custody.* The Book of Acts in First Century Setting 3. Grand Rapids: Eerdmans, 1994.

Reese, Boyd. "Apostle Paul's Exercise of His Rights as a Roman Citizen as Recorded in the Book of Acts." *Evangelical Quarterly* 47 (1975): 138–45.

Roberts, Alexander, and James Donaldson, eds. *The Ante-Nicene Fathers.* 1885–1887. 10 vols. Reprinted. Peabody: Hendrickson, 1994.

Santos, Narry F. "Intergenerational Mission in the New Testament: Examples of Life-on-Life Modeling by Jesus and Paul." In *From Womb to Tomb: Generational Missiology in the 21st Century and Beyond,* edited Sadiri Joy Tira, 47–63. Edmonton: Pagemaster Publishing, 2024.

Schäfer, Heinrich. "Fundamentalism: Power and the Absolute." *Exchange* 23, no. 1 (1994): 1–24.

Schellenberg, Ryan S. "Τὸ εν λόγω ιδιωτικὸν τοῦ Ἀποστόλου: Revisiting Patristic Testimony on Paul's Rhetorical Education." *Novum Testamentum* 54, no. 4 (2012): 354–68.

Schnabel, Eckhard J. *Acts.* Zondervan Exegetical Commentary on the New Testament. Grand Rapids: Zondervan, 2012.

Seland, Torrey. "Saul of Tarsus and Early Zealotism: Reading Gal 1:13–14 in Light of Philo's Writings." *Biblica* 83, no. 4 (2002): 449–71.

Silva, Moisés. *Philippians*. Baker Exegetical Commentary on the New Testament. Grand Rapids: Baker, 1992.
Smith, Eric C. "The Fall and Rise of Eutychus: The Church of Paul and the Spatial Habitus of Luke." *Biblical Interpretation* 28, no. 2 (2020): 228–45.
Spurgeon, Andrew B. "Practicing Hospitality: Ancient Cultural Values and the Contemporary Asian Christians." In *Exploring the New Testament in Asia: An Evangelical Perspective*. Foundations in Asian Christian Thought, edited by Samson L. Uytanlet and Bennet Lawrence, 277–97. Cumbria: Langham Global Library, 2024.
———. *Romans: A Pastoral and Contextual Commentary*. Asia Bible Commentary Series. Carlisle: Langham Global Library, 2020.
Stegemann, W. "War der Paulus ein Römischer Bürger?" *Zeitschrift für die Neutestamentliche Wissenschaft und die Kunde der Älteren Kirche* 78 (1987): 200–29.
Strabo, *Geography*. Loeb Classical Library. Translated by Horace Leonard Jones. 8 vols. Cambridge: Harvard University Press, 1917–32.
Tarn, W. W., and G. T. Griffith. *Hellenistic Civilisation*. Revised Edition. London: Meridian, 1952.
Theissen, Gerd. *The Social Setting of Pauline Christianity: Essays on Corinth*, edited and translated by John H. Schültz. Philadelphia: Fortress, 1982.
Thomas, Christine M. "At Home in the City of Artemis: Religion in Ephesos in the Literary Imagination of the Roman Period." In *Ephesos, Metropolis of Asia: An Interdisciplinary Approach to Its Archaeology, Religion, and Culture*. Harvard Theological Studies 41, edited by Helmut Koester, 81–117. Valley Forge: Trinity, 1995.
Tucker, Bram, et al. "Ethnic Markers Without Ethnic Conflict: Why Do Interdependent Masikoro, Mieka, and Vezo of Madagascar Signal Their Ethnic Differences?" *Human Nature* 32, no. 3 (2021): 529–56.
Unnik, Wilhelm C. van. *Tarsus or Jerusalem: The City of Paul's Youth*. London: Epworth Press, 1962.
Uytanlet, Juliet Lee. "Finding Home for the Unhomed: Helping Diaspora Community Discover Identity and Belonging," in *Asian Christian Theology: Evangelical Perspectives*, edited by Timoteo D. Gener and Stephen T. Pardue. Carlisle: Langham Global Library, 2019.
———. *The Hybrid Tsinoys: The Challenges of Hybridity and Homogeneity as Sociocultural Constructs Among the Chinese in the Philippines*. American Society of Missiology Monograph Series 28. Eugene: Pickwick, 2016.
Uytanlet, Samson L. "Tentmaking: Paul's Missionary Strategy?" *Evangelical Mission Quarterly* 59, no. 1 (2023): 53–55.
Uytanlet, Samson L., and Juliet Lee Uytanlet. *Manual for Sojourners: A Study on Peter's Use of Scripture and Its Relevance Today*. Eugene: Wipf and Stock, 2023.
Wenkel, David H. "The Primacy of Preaching in the Resurrection of Eutychus in Acts 20:7–12." *Biblische Notizen* 197 (2023): 95–110.
Winter, Bruce W. *After Paul Left Corinth: The Influence of Secular Ethics and Social Change*. Grand Rapids: Eerdmans, 2001.

Witherington, Ben III. *Paul Quest: The Renewed Search for the Jew of Tarsus.* Downers Grove: InterVarsity Press, 1998.

———. *The Acts of the Apostles: A Socio-Rhetorical Commentary.* Grand Rapids: Eerdmans, 1998.

Wright, N. T. *Paul and the Faithfulness of God.* Christian Origins and the Question of God 4. Minneapolis: Fortress Press, 2013.

Subject Index

A

accommodation 3, 9–10, 41, 52, 82
acculturation 9–10
Alexandria 15
Ananias
  Damascene disciple 9, 24, 31–33
  high priest 90–91, 96
Antioch
  Pisidia 41–44, 47, 69, 108
  Syria 8–9, 29, 34, 37–40, 44, 47–49, 51, 54, 76–77, 85–86
Apollos 72–74, 77
Artemis 5, 80–82
Asia
  Asia Minor (ancient) 8, 57, 59, 61, 76–78, 80–81, 85, 96
  modern 5, 14, 23, 61, 79
assimilation 9–10
Athens, Athenians 15, 17, 46, 66–70, 83, 109

B

Barnabas 9, 24, 33–34, 39–52, 54–55, 57, 77, 86–87, 111

C

circumcised 50
circumcision 4–5, 15, 17–18, 39, 43, 48, 50, 52, 54–56, 58–59, 87, 93, 96, 104, 108
citizenship 8, 12–14, 16, 21, 34, 88, 90–92, 97–99, 104
Claudius
  Claudius Lysias (commander of Roman army) 92, 95
  emperor 70
colonization, colonialism 3
Corinth, Corinthians 6, 60, 70–76, 83, 88, 100, 103, 110–11
craftsmen 4, 7, 76–77, 80–82

culture, cultural
  background xi, 8, 12, 18–19, 40, 44, 46, 52, 82
  differences 2, 4, 10, 14, 19, 38
  practices 12, 24, 59, 61, 82, 87, 93, 108
  study 2, 4, 10
  transition xi, 3, 37, 39, 60, 80
  values 3, 10, 19, 44, 86, 108
Cyprus, Cypriots
  island 34, 37–38, 40–42, 54, 57
Cyrene 37–38

D

Damascus, Damascenes 9, 28–33, 35, 39, 90, 107
diaspora
  contemporary xiii, 3, 5, 8, 18, 40, 68
  Jewish (ancient) 4–5, 7, 9–10, 14, 19–21, 27, 29, 34, 37–40, 42–46, 48, 51–52, 55, 57–62, 65, 68–71, 77–78, 82, 87–88, 90, 93, 98, 100, 104, 107–8
  various communities 3, 8, 14

E

education 6, 9–10, 14–15, 17, 21, 24, 27, 34, 58, 74, 77, 90, 108
Ephesus, Ephesians 4, 74, 76–83, 85, 88–89, 93, 95–96, 98
ethnicity
  ethnic tensions 5–6, 10, 18–19, 28, 38, 44, 52–53, 55, 57, 82, 85, 108–9, 111
  identity 5–6, 8–10, 12, 14, 17, 19, 38, 61–62, 65, 82, 108

F

false witnesses, reports 24–25, 87–89, 92–95, 98, 104, 111

Felix 13, 92–97, 100
Festus 13, 93–95, 97
finances
  benefaction 8, 14, 24, 60, 63, 70, 73, 75, 82–83, 85, 110
  economic gains and losses 4, 6, 61–62, 64, 80, 82

G
Galatia, Galatian
  people 42, 48–51, 54, 57, 66, 76–77, 85
  region 37, 40–42, 48, 59, 76
Gamaliel 9, 15, 28–29, 90, 96, 109

H
Herod Agrippa I 87
Herod Agrippa II 94–95, 97
homeless, houseless 1, 3
hospitable, hospitality xi, xiii, 1, 3–5, 31–32, 38–39, 42, 45–49, 52, 55, 57–60, 62–63, 66–68, 72, 76–78, 81–83, 85–86, 98–100, 102, 104, 108–11
hostility, inhospitality xi, xiii, 1, 3–5, 39, 55, 57, 60, 62, 64, 67–68, 70–71, 74, 76, 79, 83, 85, 87, 89, 98, 109–11

I
Iconium 44–45, 47
idol making, idol worship 4–5, 10, 49, 63, 67–68
immigrants, migration 5, 8
insurgents, insurgency 5, 13, 61, 64, 83, 92–94, 97, 109–10

J
James
  the apostle 28, 103
  the brother of Jesus 39, 87, 89, 93, 95–96
Jewish Sanhedrin 4, 26, 90–93, 97, 104
journey
  geographical 9, 21, 23, 40–41, 47, 57, 65, 77, 85–86, 90, 98
  spiritual 24, 49
Judaism 10, 24, 27, 30–31, 37–38, 41, 48–49, 76
Judaizers 48, 51, 56
John
  a.k.a. John Mark 40, 42, 54, 57, 111
  the apostle 24, 39, 53
  the Baptizer 42, 76–78

L
language
  bilingual 5, 9, 28, 38–39
  differences 5–6, 16, 21, 28, 35, 38, 40–41, 46, 53, 55, 57, 85, 108–9
  Greek 5, 28, 32, 34, 37–39, 44, 53
  Hebrew 5, 19, 28–29, 34–35, 38–39, 44, 53, 90
Lycaonia, Lycaonian
  Derbe 45, 47
  language 68
  Lystra 11, 45–47, 57–58, 82
  people 45–47, 57–59, 82, 108
Lydia
  believer 59–60, 62, 82–83, 110
  place 7, 46

M
Macedonia, Macedonian
  Berea, Bereans 65–67, 83, 109
  man from Macedonia 59
  people 14, 75, 110
  Philippi, Philippians 12–14, 59–64, 76, 82–83, 99, 110
  region 60–63, 66, 70, 76, 85
  Thessalonica, Thessalonians 5, 60, 62–67, 70, 83, 109–10
  women 64
Malta 98–99, 108

N
narcissism 72–76

O

occultism
  fortune-telling, clairvoyance 5, 12, 59, 61, 80, 82
  magic 8, 41, 79–80

P

Peter, a.k.a. Simon, Cephas xiii, 4, 24, 28, 39, 49–54, 70, 72, 78, 101
Pharisees
  religious movement 4, 9, 19, 30, 35, 52, 91, 93, 104–5, 109
  Sanhedrin 91, 93, 95
Philip 53, 86, 104
Phoenicia, Phoenicians 37, 51–52
Phrygia 7, 42, 59, 76–77
power
  abuse xi, 12–13, 25, 70–71, 89–94, 104, 107, 109, 111–12
  gaining and losing influence 4, 32–33, 35, 43, 55–57, 60, 64, 66–67, 77, 82, 85, 104–5, 107, 109–11
  gaining and losing power 3–4, 6, 92–94, 98, 107, 111
  God's empowerment 103
  misinformation 87, 111
  political power and standing 5–6, 19–20, 35, 65, 83, 85, 92, 94, 97, 105, 108, 110
  powerlessness 90, 105
prejudice 49
priesthood
  elites 4
  of believers 101
  religious leaders 9, 15, 26, 28–29, 31, 90–91, 93–94, 96–97
  Sadducees 4, 24, 90, 105
  Sanhedrin 26, 96–97
  temple of Zeus 46
Priscilla and Aquila 70, 72, 74, 100–1
prison, imprisonment 4–5, 12–13, 24, 27, 59–60, 62, 82, 85–86, 88–92, 94–95, 98–100, 103–4, 108
proselytes, proselytism 17, 20, 38–39, 41–44, 48–49, 52–53, 59, 64, 66, 68, 70, 108–9
psychoanalysis 2

R

religion
  background 6, 17–18, 21, 58, 80, 85, 108
  identity 8, 23, 77, 108
  Jewish groups 4, 23–28, 30, 35, 57, 72, 77, 87–88, 90, 93, 95, 98
  power 23–28, 33, 35, 87, 90, 92, 95, 98, 105, 108–9, 111
  practice, piety 7, 12, 15, 19–21, 23–24, 33, 37, 49, 54, 59, 61, 63, 69, 81, 87, 93, 107–8
  violence, persecution 4–6, 9, 13, 20–21, 23–29, 31–35, 37, 39, 43–45, 47, 51, 57, 61, 64–68, 71, 83, 86–92, 94, 96–97, 104–5, 107, 109–11
  zeal 20–21, 23–24, 27, 29, 31–35, 37, 39, 43, 49, 57, 67, 87–93, 96–97, 107, 109
Roman custody 89–90, 92, 94, 100, 103
Roman Empire 13, 15, 59, 62

S

Samaria, Samaritans 5, 29, 37, 51–53, 55, 60, 78
shipwreck 98, 108
Silas 12, 54, 57–66, 72
Stephen 9, 24–26, 28, 37, 42, 45, 51, 85
synagogues (Jewish diaspora) 5, 28–32, 34, 38–39, 42–44, 46, 49, 58–60, 63–66, 70–72, 76, 78, 96

T

Tarsus 8–9, 15–16, 19, 21, 33–34, 39, 42, 77, 85, 87, 90, 96
tentmaker 9, 14, 70, 76
theology, theological
  doctrinal differences 4, 6, 24, 37, 48, 52, 57, 66, 83, 85, 91, 105, 109

education 10, 83
reflections 9
training 86
the Way 39, 78, 107
Timothy 57–62, 72, 82
Titus 11, 50, 58, 89

U
"unhomely" (Bhabha) xiii, 2
"unhomely," "uncanny" (Freud) 2

V
various communities 8

W
wealth and social status 4–6, 12, 14, 75, 81–83, 85, 107–8, 110–11

Author Index

A
Augustine 16

B
Barclay, John M. G. 9–10
Betz, Hans Dieter 30
Bhabha, Homi K. xiii, 2–3
Bruce, F. F. 25–26, 28, 68

C
Chilton, Bruce 49
Chrysostom, John 16

D
Deissmann, Adolf 11

E
Eusebius 103

F
Freud, Sigmund 2–3

G
George, Roji Thomas 19
Gier, Nicholas F. 23
Girma, Hewan 8
Gruen, Erich S. 51, 59

I
Irenaeus 16

J
John Chrysostom 16
Josephus 7–8, 13, 15, 62, 87

K
Keener, Craig S. 28, 34, 43, 52, 97

O
Ortega, Gema 40

P
Philo 20, 25, 88
Pliny 67

R
Ramsay, William M. 17

S
Schnabel, Eckhard J. 60
Seland, Torrey 20
Strabo 8, 15–16

W
Witherington, Ben, III 20
Wright, N. T. 50, 101–2

Scripture Index

OLD TESTAMENT

Genesis
14:13 19
17:12 18
17:14 18
34:1–31 55
34:15 55

Exodus
19:6 101

Leviticus
12:3 18
18:1–30 74
24:16 25

Numbers
6:1–21 87
6:18 87
15:35 25
25:7–13 20

Deuteronomy
6:1–2 15
13:17 1

Joshua
8:28 1
13:3 1
18:21–28 19

Judges
8:24 18

1 Samuel
9:1–2 18
10:1 18
16:7 12

2 Samuel
7:5–6 25
25:13 26
30:24 26

1–2 Kings 7

1 Kings
6:11–13 25
8:27 25
8:30 25
8:39 25
8:43 25
8:49 25
12:21 19
19:18 71

2 Kings
24:14–16 7

2 Chronicles
6:2 25
6:18 25
6:21 25
6:30 25
6:33 25
6:39 25
36:15 25
36:20–21 7

Ezra
7:10 20
9:13–15 108
10:2 108
10:10 108
10:17–18 108

Nehemiah
13:27 108

Job
8:14 1

Psalms
106:30 20

Isaiah
42:6 .... 30, 101
43:21 101
49:6 101
53:2 11
60:3 101

Jeremiah
1:5 30
25:11–12 7
29:10 7

Daniel
9:2 7

Hosea
13:5 1

NEW TESTAMENT

Matthew
3:11 77
5:21–48 20
10:14 44
22:21 110
23:15 20
27:32 37
27:40 24
28:19 101

Mark
1:7 77
3:6 20
5:28 79
6:11 44
7:18–19 10
8:15 20
12:13 20
12:17 110
14:58 24
15:21 37

Luke
1:52 28
2:32 .... 30, 101
2:52 12
4:24 34
9:5 44
10:11 44
11:48 27
13:1–2 61
19:3 12
20:25 110
22:26 112
22:30 28
22:49–53 20
23:6 61
23:26 37

John 4
1:15–30 77
2:19 25
4 5

4:9 55
4:44 34
16:2–3 20

Acts
1:8 .... 43, 52
2 53
2:5 52
2:10 70
2:39 53
4:8–18 24
4:10 4
4:10–20 99
4:13 24
4:14–16 24
4:16 24
4:17–18 24
4:36 40
5:34–39 28
6 .... 5, 34, 53
6:1 .... 5, 19, 38, 44
6:1–7 28
6–7 9
6:9 34
6:11–14 24
6:13 24
6:14 24
7:1–47 25
7:2–3 52
7–9 29
7:9–10 52
7:10 52
7:48–49 25
7:49 25
7:50–53 25
7:54 25–26
7:56 24–25
7:57 25
7:58 26
7:58–8:1 9
7:58–8:3 8
8:1 .... 26–27, 29, 37, 51, 86

8:3 .... 9, 27
8:4 27
8:4–5 27
8–11 32
8:14–17 53
8:14–18 78
8:25 53
8:26–40 53
9:1–2 .... 9, 28, 89
9:1–18 71
9:1–31 8
9:2 33
9:3 29
9:4 29
9:5 29
9:6 30
9:7 29
9:8 29
9:10–17 31
9:11 9
9:13 31
9:15 30
9:15–16 31
9:17 31
9:18–19 .... 31, 33
9:19–22 32
9:20 .... 30, 33
9:21 .... 29, 31
9:22 .... 32–33, 39
9:23 32–33
9:26 33–34
9:26–27 39
9:26–30 9
9:26–31 .... 39, 86–87
9:27 33
9:27–29 39
9:28 34
9:29 34
9:30 34
10 53
10:1–43 53
10:9–33 54
10:9–48 49

10:44–48 53	13:45 42–43	16:9 59
11:1–18 54	13:46 44	16:13 59
11:19 .... 27, 29, 37, 51	13:46–49 43	16:14 60
11:19–20 38	13:47 .... 30, 43, 101	16:14–15 82
11:19–20 44	13:47–48 69	16:15 83
11:20 40	13:50 43	16:16–19 61
11:22–24 39	13:50–51 47	16:19–24 .... 5, 82
11:25 34	13:51 44	16:20–21 12
11:25–26 39	14:1 44	16:21 61
11:25–30 8	14:2 44	16:22–23 12
11:26 39	14:3 45	16:23–24 62
11:27–30 86	14:5 45	16:24 62
12:1–3 103	14:5–7 .... 45, 47	16:25–26 62
12:1–5 28	14:8–12 45	16:27–32 62
12:17 28	14:11 46	16:33 62
12:25 86	14:11–13 .... 58, 108	16:36 12
13 41	14:12 45–46	16:37–40 13
13:1–3 .... 9, 40	14:13 46	16:40 60
13:1–9 8	14:15 46	17 67
13:4 34	14:15–17 46	17:2 63
13:4–5 40	14:17 68	17:3 63
13:5 40	14:18 46	17:4 64
13:6–8 41	14:19 47	17:5 66
13:9 .... 8, 40–41	14:21–23 47	17:5–7 64
13:9–10 56	14:22 47	17:7 .... 64, 83, 109
13:10 41	14:24–27 40	17:10 65
13:12 41	14:26–28 76	17:11 .... 65, 109
13:13 .... 40, 42, 86	14:27 48	17:12 .... 43, 65
13:13–39 108	14:28 .... 40, 47	17:13 66
13:13–52 42	15 56	17:16 68
13:14 42	15:1 93	17:17 66–68
13:14–41 46	15:2 .... 51, 86	17:19–21 66
13:15 42–43	15:3 51	17:20 64
13:16 69	15:5 .... 48, 52, 93, 109	17:21 67
13:16–22 42	15:7–12 .... 52, 54	17:22 69
13:17 69	15:22–35 93	17:22–32 46
13:17–19 69	15:36 54	17:23 68
13:23–41 42	15:37–38 54	17:23–24 69
13:30–34 69	15:39 .... 34, 54, 57	17:24 68
13:33–38 69	15:40–41 .... 54, 57	17:26 69
13:36 43	16:1 82	17:26–27 68–69
13:38–39 69	16:3 59	17:28 69
13:40–41 69	16:6 59	17:29 109
13:42–43 42	16:6–7 .... 61, 76, 86	17:30–31 69
13:44 43	16:7 59	17:31–32 69

17:32 67	20:2 81–82	22:25–26 13
18:1 70	20:3 81	22:27–29 13
18:2 .... 70, 100–1	20:6 81	22:28 .... 12, 14
18:4 70	20:12 82	22:30–23:11 89
18:5 72	20:16 .... 81, 86	23:2–4 93
18:6a 70	20:33–35 63	23:2–5 90
18:6b 70	20:38 82	23:4 91
18:7–8 .... 70, 72	21:3 85	23:6 .... 91, 96
18:8 70	21:4 85	23:6–8 .... 4, 24
18:9–10 71	21:6 86	23:6–10 93
18:11 .... 76, 81	21:7 85	23:7–10 91
18:12–13 71	21:8 .... 86, 104	23:9 95
18:13 88	21:11 86	23:10 92
18:13–15 71	21:12–13 86	23:11 .... 92, 96
18:14–15 88	21:20–21 .... 87–90, 96	23:12 89
18:17 71–72	21:21 .... 93, 104	23:12–22 91
18:18 .... 76, 87	21:22–24 .... 93, 96	23:23 91
18:19 76	21:23–24 .... 87, 89	23:23–26:32 89
18:20 76	21:24 95	23:27 92
18:21 76	21:27 .... 88, 93	23:27–28 92
18:23 76	21:27–22:29 89	23:29 .... 92, 95
18:24–19:1 74	21:27–32 95	23:30 92
18:24–28 72	21:28 96	24:2 92
18:25 77	21:28–29 93	24:5 .... 93, 96
19:4 77	21:28–30 88	24:5–6 93
19:5 77	21:31–32 88	24:6 96
19:6 78	21:31–36 89	24:10–12 96
19:7 77	21:37–22:21 89	24:15 96
19:8 78	21:37–38 13	24:17–18 96
19:9 78	21:39 19	24:18–19 95
19:9–10 78	21:40 .... 19, 39	24:18–21 96
19:10 81	22:2 .... 19, 39, 90	24:22 94–95
19:11 79	22:3 .... 8, 14–15, 96	24:23 .... 94–95, 99
19:11–2 79	22:3–5 43	24:24 95
19:12 79	22:3–5 90	24:25 94
19:18–19 80	22:4–5 96	24:26 .... 94–95, 97
19:18–20 83	22:6 29	24:26–27 13
19:21 96	22:7 29	24:27 .... 94, 100
19:21–20:1 81	22:8 29	25:2–3 .... 93–94, 97
19:24–27 82	22:9 29	25:7 97
19:25–27 .... 4, 80	22:21 96	25:8 97
19:28–41 82	22:22 96	25:8–12 94
19:32 81	22:23–25 92	25:9 .... 94, 97–98
19:40 81	22:23–29 95	25:10–11 97
20:1 81	22:25 90	25:10–12 13

25:12 ....94, 97	**Romans**	5:2 75
25:13–17 94	1:8–15 100	7:29–31 10
25:18 ....94–95, 97	1:15 ....59, 96	7:39 10
25:19 97	2:19–20 102	8–10 10
25:21 94	3:1–8 102	9:1–18 73
26:4–11 97	5:10–11 102	9:21 9
26:5 14	5:20 102	9:22 55
26:13 29	7 10	11:18–21 75
26:14 ....19, 29	8:15–17 41	11:22 75
26:16–18 30	8:23 41	11:27 75
26:18 30	8:26 112	12:1–31 74
26:23 30	9–11 102	13:4 74
26:31 95	9–11 101	15:14 77
26:32 ....13, 94, 97	9:30–33 101	15:32 81
27 98	11:12 102	16:20 10
27:3 98–99	11:15 102	
27:7 99	11:22–24 102	**2 Corinthians**
27:11 98	13:1 110	2:1–11 75
27:16 99	14:1–3 102	4:7–12 xii
27:20 99	15:18–19 100	5:6 63
27:30 98	15:19 59	5:6–9 103–4
27:33 99	15:19–20 77	5:8 63
27:37 98	15:22–23 100	7:8–12 75
27:43 98	15:22–24 59	8:1–3 63
28:1–2 98	16:1–16 100	8:1–5 75
28:1–10 108	16:16 10	9:1–15 75
28:3 99		10:1–2 73
28:4–6 99	**1 Corinthians**	10:10 ....12, 17, 74
28:7 99	1–4 10	11:1–12:21 74
28:7–10 99	1:11 73	11:6 ....10, 17, 74
28:11 99	1:11–12 73	11:9 ....60, 110
28:12 99	1:11–13 72	11:23–27 103
28:13 99	1:12 73	11:30 17
28:14 99	1:17 17	11:32–33 33
28:18 ....95, 100	1:26–27 73	12:5 17
28:21–24 93	2:1–5 73	12:7–10 xii
28:22–23 99	2:3 17	12:9 ....17, 103, 112
28:23 101	3:1–3 71	12:10 6
28:24–26 101	3:1–23 72	
28:24–28 100	3:3 74	**Galatians**
28:28 101	4:3 73	1:5 30
28:30 99–100	4:7 73–74	1:6 50
28:30–31 ....100, 103	4:13 73	1:8–9 ....51, 66
49:6 30	4:16 72	1:12 ....49, 109
	5:1 74	1:13–14 ....20, 27, 49

1:15–16 30
1:16 50
1:17–19 50
2:1–2 .... 50, 109
2:3 .... 50, 58
2:7–9 50
2:8–9 11
2:9 39
2:11–14 54
2:12 10
2:20 112
3:14 50
3:26–28 .... xi, 50
4:4–7 41
5:1–15 50
5:6 50
16:3 58

Ephesians
1:3 79
1:19–23 79
2:14–18 xi
6:10–20 79

Philippians
1:5 110
1:5–7 60
1:5–17 99
1:21 112
3:1–11 xii
3:5 .... 15, 17–20
3:6 .... 20, 23, 89
3:7 23
3:7–10 107
4:2–3 60
4:10–19 60
4:11 10
4:12 14
4:13 112
4:15 110
4:15–16 63
4:16 63

Colossians
2:1–5 100
3:3 xii
3:8 100
3:11 xi
4:10 111

1 Thessalonians
1:8 63
1:9 63
1:9–10 63
2:1–2 63
2:7–8 63
2:9 .... 63, 112
2:14–15 65
4:11 63
4:16 60
5:12 .... 63, 112
5:12–14 63
17:7 5

2 Thessalonians
1:9 63
2:2 .... 63, 66
3:6–12 63
3:7–8 63

2 Timothy
1:5 58
4:6 103–4
4:7 .... 104, 112
4:8 104
4:11 111
4:16–17 103
4:17 103
4:18 103

Hebrews
11:9 xii
11:10 xii
13:2 46
13:14–15 xii

1 Peter
2:9 101

Jude
3 109

Revelation
5:9 53
13:7 53
14:6 53

Langham Literature and its imprints are a ministry of Langham Partnership.

Langham Partnership is a global fellowship working in pursuit of the vision God entrusted to its founder John Stott –

> *to facilitate the growth of the church in maturity and Christ-likeness through raising the standards of biblical preaching and teaching.*

Our vision is to see churches in the Majority World equipped for mission and growing to maturity in Christ through the ministry of pastors and leaders who believe, teach and live by the word of God.

Our mission is to strengthen the ministry of the word of God through:
- nurturing national movements for biblical preaching
- fostering the creation and distribution of evangelical literature
- enhancing evangelical theological education

especially in countries where churches are under-resourced.

Our ministry

Langham Preaching partners with national leaders to nurture indigenous biblical preaching movements for pastors and lay preachers all around the world. With the support of a team of trainers from many countries, a multi-level programme of seminars provides practical training, and is followed by a programme for training local facilitators. Local preachers' groups and national and regional networks ensure continuity and ongoing development, seeking to build vigorous movements committed to Bible exposition.

Langham Literature provides Majority World preachers, scholars and seminary libraries with evangelical books and electronic resources through publishing and distribution, grants and discounts. The programme also fosters the creation of indigenous evangelical books in many languages, through writer's grants, strengthening local evangelical publishing houses, and investment in major regional literature projects, such as one volume Bible commentaries like *The Africa Bible Commentary* and *The South Asia Bible Commentary*.

Langham Scholars provides financial support for evangelical doctoral students from the Majority World so that, when they return home, they may train pastors and other Christian leaders with sound, biblical and theological teaching. This programme equips those who equip others. Langham Scholars also works in partnership with Majority World seminaries in strengthening evangelical theological education. A growing number of Langham Scholars study in high quality doctoral programmes in the Majority World itself. As well as teaching the next generation of pastors, graduated Langham Scholars exercise significant influence through their writing and leadership.

To learn more about Langham Partnership and the work we do visit **langham.org**

www.ingramcontent.com/pod-product-compliance
Lightning Source LLC
Chambersburg PA
CBHW050829160426
43192CB00010B/1955